THOMAS BUTLER

and

HIS DESCENDENTS

A Genealogy of the Descendants of
Thomas and Elizabeth Butler
of
Butler's Hill
South Berwick, Maine

1674 *to* 1886

George H. Butler, M.D.

HERITAGE BOOKS
2008

HERITAGE BOOKS

AN IMPRINT OF HERITAGE BOOKS, INC.

Books, CDs, and more—Worldwide

For our listing of thousands of titles see our website
at
www.HeritageBooks.com

A Facsimile Reprint
Published 2008 by
HERITAGE BOOKS, INC.
Publishing Division
100 Railroad Ave. #104
Westminster, Maryland 21157

Originally published
New York
Trow's Printing and Bookbinding Company
201-213 East Twelfth Street
1886

International Standard Book Numbers
Paperbound: 978-1-55613-241-4
Clothbound: 978-0-7884-7253-4

PREFACE.

THIS short contribution to family history, the fruits of leisure moments occurring in a busy professional life during the past ten years—requiring an extensive correspondence and much research among ancient records and documents—deals with facts rather than panegyrics. The object has been to put in enduring form the genealogical records of the family, a task which every decade renders more difficult, and which, in many instances, has proven not an easy one. No eulogies have been indulged in, and doubtless in many cases where members have filled positions of honor or of trust, no mention has been made of such facts, because those most interested have not thought it of sufficient importance to furnish the necessary data.

It will be readily seen that in a work of this nature, where so many dates are recorded, errors will creep in—are in fact almost unavoidable. And although great pains have been taken to verify all dates and other facts in the present work, doubtless it contains its share. This no one can possibly regret more than the author.

While the author is not one of those who consign

to the "limbo" of the waste-basket, as totally un-
worthy of credence or consideration, all tradition,
yet in this work, to unsupported traditions no weight
has been given; and the following traditions, "that
of three brothers who came from Ireland together,
Thomas settled in Kittery about 1698, while of the
others one went to Connecticut and the other
South;" another, "that Thomas was a shipmaster
and came to Kittery in his own vessel;" and a third,
"that he came influenced by the advice of his friend
John Wentworth," are only mentioned here because
they are so generally believed. While either of
these traditions are probable, there is no proof of
any of them. They rest on the merest tradition.

Although it has never been questioned, and there
is no doubt of its truth, yet in the absence of the
exact date of his birth and parish records, positive
proof of the descent of Thomas [1] Butler from the
house of Ormond, and his right to the following
arms, viz.: *Arms*, Or, a chief indented az.; *crest*, in a
ducal coronet, Or, a plume of five ostrich feathers,
Ar., thereon a falcon rising of the last—is impos-
sible.

The author will esteem it a favor on the part of
any reader who will send to his address, No. 42
East Sixty-sixth Street, New York City, the facts
to correct any error or omission which they may
discover, or any information which will help to fill
any hiatus in this work.

ERRATA AND CORRIGENDA.

Page 43, line 12, for "Phineas [6] Hanson (277) died without issue," read, "had William [7] Hanson, died without issue." Line 19, omit, "279. III. Lydia [6] Hanson, born in Berwick."

Page 46, line 11, for "Elizabeth Jane Hall," read, "Elizabeth Jane Fall."

Page 139, line 11, for "Sarah [5] (1466)" read, "(1490)."

DESCENDANTS OF THOMAS BUTLER.

I. THOMAS BUTLER was born about 1674. He signed an affidavit in 1733, stating his age to be fifty-nine years; this is all that is certainly known regarding his age. He was of that numerous family of Butlers descended from the house of Ormond. The exact date when he settled in Berwick is not definitely known; but that he was here as early as 1698 with his wife Elizabeth appears by the certificate of the birth of their son Thomas, contained in the town "Records" of Kittery, March 6, 1698.

Mr. Butler was a leading citizen of Berwick, and acted a prominent part in the affairs of the town for more than twenty-five years. Where he was educated is not positively known; but that he was a gentleman with fair pretensions to some degree of scholarly attainments seems evident from the fact of his ability, among other attainments, to teach the Latin language. In 1716 it was found difficult to engage a satisfactory teacher for the parish school, and one who could teach the Latin language, or, as expressed by one of the Board of

Selectmen, one who "had the Latin tongue." So, in compliance with the following resolution, he taught the parish school until a satisfactory arrangement could be made with some other— "Voted, Mr. Thomas Butler to be schoolmaster until another be provided." There is no evidence that he ever received any compensation for his services as teacher, although he taught the school during the greater part of this year. He was at the same time one of the Board of Selectmen and Surveyor of Lands.

He was possessed of ample means for the times in which he lived, and maintained a style of living befitting one who numbered among his intimate friends and associates such well-known names as Governor Wentworth, Sir William Pepperell, Hon. John Hill, Captain Ichabod Plaisted, Humphrey Chadbourne, etc.

The following extract from the "Records of Kittery" show that he first received a grant of land, May 24, 1699, "at a legal town meeting held at Kittery, May 24, 1699. Lt. John Shapleigh was chosen moderator for the said day, John Heard, Joshua Downing, and Joseph Wilson were chosen to sit with ye Selectmen, for to allow of all grants of land that be granted this day. Here follows a list of ye several persons that had lands granted to them this day, with ye number of acres. Granted Thomas Butler 21 acres."

Although Berwick was not set off to be a separate parish from Kittery until 1701, yet a settlement of no insignificant importance was established where the village of South Berwick now stands at a very early date in the history of the colonies (in fact, an early historian of America states Berwick to have been the thirty-fourth town settled in New England), attracted here, no doubt, by the advantages afforded by the numerous and abundant falls in the Salmon Falls and Great Works rivers, yielding an abundance of water-power for saw-mills and grain-mills. Here was also the head of navigation for small vessels, all-essential, and affording ample means for the procuring, manufacturing, and transportation of lumber and ship-timber. And as the lumbering and timber interests were among the most important occupations of the State, at that time, this settlement promised to grow speedily to the proportions of a thriving village. It was here that this first grant of land to him was located, but he never occupied it as a residence.

He soon after acquired a large tract of land in South Berwick, to the east of the village, comprising the lands now occupied by the academy, Butler's Hill, those now covered by a part of the village, and the land owned and occupied by Hiram Butler at the present time. Here, just at the foot of this hill, which has ever since borne his name, he built for himself a substantial and spacious two-story double house, where he ever after resided and dispensed generous hospitality. This house has since been removed, and its site is now occupied by a more modern structure, the residence of Dr. Trafton.

As has been stated, Berwick was, by an act of the General Court, set off as a separate parish, with powers to elect selectmen and other officers for its local government, and to employ a minister for its church, and a teacher for its parish school; yet it was not until 1713 that by an act of the General Court it became a distinct town.

On the 12th day of August, 1712, Captain John Hill was elected " to represent this parish at the Great and General Court to be held at Boston, the 20th current, or at the next session relating to the division of Lower Kittery from this parish, &c." And on the 9th of June, following, the act was passed by the General Court, " Ordering that Berwick be a distinct and separate town, and shall have and enjoy all immunities and privileges as other towns do by law enjoy, &c. &c." This act was accepted and ratified by vote in legal town meeting held September 9, 1714, and at a legal town meeting held the following 22d of March, 1714/15, James Emery, James Grant, Elisha Plaisted, and Thomas Butler were elected selectmen of the town for the ensuing year.

The next year he was elected one of the Board of Selectmen, a grand juror, and schoolmaster. Besides other offices filled by him he served in the capacity of selectman from 1714/15 to 1726/27, inclusive, with the exception of three years, viz., 1717/18,

1721/22. It was probably due to his being a good mathematical scholar that he was annually elected surveyor of lands from 1713 to 1736, inclusive, when he saw both of his sons elected to that office in his place, and it was in this capacity that his character as careful and painstaking is most apparent. It was his custom to preserve copies of his surveys ; and for this purpose he had a large sheepskin reduced to parchment, on which he made drawings of his surveys. These were continued by his son Thomas, and this chart has proved quite useful to surveyors of the present time as a reference for the purpose of verifying courses, where ancient landmarks have become obliterated. It was the property of his great-great-grandson, David G. Butler,[5] of Great Falls, N. H., until recently, when it was borrowed for the purpose of verifying some surveys and never returned.

Although Mr. Butler did not become a member of the church until the 2d day of September, 1727, when he owned the covenant and was baptized, he was appointed to employ ministers of the church and given full powers to " settle with them as to their salaries." He was ever among the foremost in any measure tending to promote the interests of the community in which he lived. This is especially evinced by the interest he manifested in the schools, and in the improvements to the navigation of the river. For the latter he gave both time and money.

In 1720 we find him recorded as one of a committee elected to settle the disputes (which were long standing) arising between Berwick and Kittery in the division of lands (these disputes had lasted ever since the division of Berwick from Kittery). On March 3d, 1729/30, the town having voted to raise the amount of money falling to its share necessary for the maintenance of the agent of the house of representatives of this province at the court of Great Britain," and not being able to raise the money needed, until a new rate was taken, we find him, with his son Moses, John Hill, Humphrey Chadbourne, Elisha Plaisted, Peter and James Grant, and others, recorded as voluntarily making up the sum; to be paid them when the rate should be made and the money collected. During his life Mr. Butler was elected to office more than thirty-five times. He was owner of a considerable property in lands and in the mills in Quamphegan. His wife died December 2d, 1728, and was buried in the old burying-ground in South Berwick, and her head-stone, the oldest in the grounds, is still standing, with the following inscription: "Here lies y° body of Mrs. Elizabeth Butler, died December y° 2, 1728."

The date of his death I have not been able to find. He was living and elected to office as late as 1736, which is the last public mention I find of him.

Their children were

2. I. THOMAS,[2] born in South Berwick, March 6, 1698.

3. II. ELIZABETH,[2] born in South Berwick, September 22, 1699.

4. III. Moses,[2] born in South Berwick, July 13, 1702.

5. IV. Abigail,[2] baptized an adult, February 18, 1719/20.

6. V. Love,[2] born in South Berwick, July 10, 1713, baptized August 16, 1713.

2.

THOMAS,[2] first child of Thomas[1] and Elizabeth Butler, was born March 6, 1698, and baptized August 14, 1720. He is first mentioned in the town "Records" of Berwick in 1725, when he was elected constable. In 1735 he was elected surveyor of lands, and continued to be elected to the latter office for several years. He held other offices of the town. His occupation was that of a manufacturer of and trader in timber and lumber.

Mr. Butler was a large landowner, and had a considerable property in the Quamphegan Mills. He inherited the homestead of his father, "Butler's Hill," where he lived and died. He is described in old documents as gentleman. He bequeathed his property according to the following will:

"In the name of God, Amen. I, Thomas Butler, of Berwick, in the county of York, Gent[n], the twelfth day of February, 1759, being very sick and weak of body, but of perfect mind & memory. Thanks be given unto God.

"Therefore, calling unto mind the mortality of my body, and knowing that it is appointed for all men once to die, do make and ordain this my last will & testament, that is to say, principally and first of all, I give & recommend my soul into the hands of God that gave it, and my body I recommend to the earth, to be buried in decent christian burial at y[e] discretion of my executors, nothing doubting but at the General Resurrection I shall receive the same again by the mighty power of God. And as touching such worldly Estate wherewith it hath pleased God to bless me in this life, I give, demise & dispose of y[e] same in y[e] follow[g] manner and form.

"Imp[e] I give to my well beloved wife all my household goods & personal estate.,

"I give to my beloved son Moses Butler one third part of my homestead with half the house thereon; and also one third part of a lot of Land at Blackberry Hill, he paying one third part of the following Legacies or Bequests when he shall arrive to the years of twenty-one.

"Item. I give & bequeath to my son Thomas Butler thirteen pounds six shillings & eight-pence.

"Item. I give to my daughter Olive Fippenny Forty Shillings.

"Item. I give to my daughter Elizabeth Sayward Forty shillings.

"Item. I give to my grandson William Goodwin the son of my daughter Mary Dec[d] twenty Shillings.

"Item. I give to my beloved son Samuel Butler,

whom I likewise constitute, make & ordain my sole
Executor of this my last will & testament, the two
thirds part of my homestead, and half my dwelling
house & Barn, the two thirds parts of a lot of Land
at Blackberry Hill, also all my right in the Mills in
Quamphegan & privilege, and ten acres of timber
land in the woods, he paying y⁰ Two thirds parts of
the above Legacys and all my just Debts & funeral
charges."

He had by wife Mehitable:

7. I. MARY,³ baptized in South Berwick, July 17,
1726. She married ——— Goodwin and had

8. I. WILLIAM⁴ GOODWIN, mentioned in his grandfather Thomas'² will.

9. II. OLIVE,³ baptized in South Berwick, March
31, 1728, is mentioned in her father's will as
wife of ——— Fippenny.

10. III. THOMAS,³ baptized in South Berwick, February 15, 1729/30.

11. IV. ELIZABETH,³ baptized in South Berwick, September 12, 1731, is mentioned in her father's will
as wife of ——— Sayward.

12. V. SAMUEL,³ baptized in South Berwick, May
19, 1734.

13. VI. ICHABOD,³ baptized in South Berwick, January 4, 1737.

14. VII. MOSES,³ baptized in South Berwick, February 28, 1741/2.

3.

ELIZABETH,[2] second child of Thomas[1] and Elizabeth Butler, born in South Berwick, September 22, 1699, married, in Berwick, December 22, 1722, Thomas Goodwin; they had.

15. I. HENRY[3] GOODWIN, baptized in South Berwick, November 21, 1723.

16. II. SUSANNAH[3] GOODWIN, baptized in South Berwick, May 23, 1725.

17. III. DANIEL[3] GOODWIN, baptized in South Berwick, December 25, 1726.

18. IV. GIDEON[3] GOODWIN, baptized in South Berwick, July 24, 1729.

19. V. GIDEON[3] GOODWIN again, baptized October 5, 1732.

20. VI. THOMAS[3] GOODWIN, baptized with Gideon.

4.

CAPTAIN MOSES,[2] third child of Thomas[1] and Elizabeth Butler, born July 13, 1702, is first mentioned in official life in 1730 in connection with the seizure of logs belonging to certain of the inhabitants of Berwick, by the King's surveyor of woods.

As early as 1668 the Governor of Massachusetts had reserved " all white pine trees of twenty-four inches in diameter at three feet above the ground for the public use."

In King William's reign a surveyor of woods

had been appointed by the Crown, and an order sent to the Earl of Bellomont to cause acts to be passed in his several governments for the preservation of the white pine trees, and in 1708 a law was made in New Hampshire prohibiting the cutting of such white pine trees as were twenty-four inches in diameter at twelve inches above the ground, without leave of the surveyor, who was instructed by the Queen to mark with the broad arrow all such trees as were or might be fit for the use of the Navy and to keep a register of them. The rigid execution of the office of Surveyor-General had always been attended with difficulties; and the violent manner in which Major Dunbar proceeded with alleged trespassers raised a spirit of opposition on such occasions.

The statutes for the preservation of the woods empowered the Surveyor to seize all logs cut from white pine trees without a license ; and it rested on the claimant to prove his property in the court of admiralty.

Dunbar went to saw-mills, where he seized and marked large quantities of lumber; and with an air and manner to which he had been accustomed in his military capacity, abused and threatened the people. That class of men with whom he was disposed to contend are not easily intimidated with high words, and he was not a match for them in that species of controversy which they denominated swamp law."

The frequent and arbitary seizure by the "Surveyor-General" " of both logs and lumber wherever found, and the contemptuous manner with which he met all remonstrances coupled with the trouble and expense of proving property when once seized, and often at a distance from the place of seizure, finally aroused such a spirit of resistance that we find the following on record : " At a legal town meeting held at Berwick, April 18, 1729, voted money shall be raised of this town for the defending any person or persons belonging to this town of Berwick who have had any logs seized by the surveyor which were cut within this township."

Also, " Voted sixty pounds shall be raised forthwith to defray the charges of carrying on that affair."

This was not only a delicate affair, but one of vital interest to this community, so dependent on the timber interests, which were among the principal occupations at this time, and especially at this juncture, when the case had been tried in the courts, and the findings of the court recorded against the claimants, and the difficulties were further enhanced by complaints both openly and covertly of the administration at Boston accusing the Governor of failing to bring to punishment such as were found cutting timber without a license. The next August, the following appears on the town "Records : " " At a legal town meeting held at Berwick, August 3, 1730, voted Capt. Elisha Plaisted, Benj. Libby, Joseph Chadbourne, John Thompson, Moses Hubbard, and Moses Butler, a committee in this matter, &c." Mr. Butler was chosen by this committee to represent them in these matters, and to attend at the General Court in Boston. He seems to have been successful in this undertaking, and by vote of the town was paid his expenses, and in 1733 was elected to the board of selectmen of Berwick, and continued to be re-elected annually till 1737. He was also chosen surveyor of lands in 1734, and continued in this office until 1756. He was selectman again from 1747 to 1756, being this year chosen moderator of town meeting.

The date of his first commission as Captain is not known, but it must have been before 1740, as this year we find Capt. Moses Butler voted one of a committee "to set off a parish from Berwick." When it was resolved to fit out an expedition to Cape Breton against the Fortress of Louisberg, in 1744, Berwick was among the first to catch the spirit, and here as elsewhere the enthusiasm ran very high; and Capt. Butler was among the first to re-cruit his company, which was the seventh company of the first Massachusetts regiment (under the command of Sir Wm. Pepperell), which he commanded during the remarkable siege and capture of this strong fortress, sharing with his men alike the depriva-tions and hardships of a winter siege and the joys at the closing victory. His commission in this service is dated February 5, 1744. The following is a copy of a letter from Sir William Pepperell to John

Hill, Esq., communicated by N. J. Herrick, Esq., to the *N. E. Hist. Gen. Register*, and published in the July number, 1869 :

DEAR SIR :—The day last past I heard that Capt. Butler had enlisted in Berwick his fifty brave sol^{drs}. This news was like a cordial to me, to hear that Berwick, Brother to Kittery, my own native town, had such a brave English spirit. I received last night a letter from ye Honor^{ble} Committee of War, who write that they tho^t there was upon our making up five or six companys of our brave county of York men. Y^e full number that was proposed all enlisted, & more, so that there will be a number clear^d off, but you may assure yourself that our brave county of York men shall not be clear^d of without they desire it. Speak to Capt. Butler to hasten down, for I have some Enlisting money sent me for him. I am sorry that some of your Commission Officers in your town seem to be uneasy because they had not had ye offer of a commission in this Expedition ; I understand you spoke to them ; did they expect that at this time I should have waited on them ? I think if they had ye least inclination to have gone, I think it was their Duty they owed to God, their King & Country, to come and offer theirselves. My love to ye Lady and all inquiring Friends.

I am your affectionate Friend & Servt,

W^m. PEPPERELL.

I don't doubt in ye least but the Commission Officers in Berwick are Brave, good men as any in this Province, and would willingly venture their lives with their coll^s, &c. I believe that nothing would now hinder them but their business in going on as ye intended Expedition, therefore I excuse them willingly; please to tell them all I sincerely value & love them, & that if there should be occasion for forces to be sent after us I don't doubt in ye least but they will be ready to come when their business is over. I beg all their prayers.

Dear Brother I wish you well,

W. P.

[Addressed on His Majes^{ty} Services | To the Honor^{ble} | John Hill, Esq. | att. | Berwick.]

He was in Louisberg, July 4, 1745, when he with other members of his company signed a power of attorney to Lieutenant Peter Grant to receive their bounty money.

In 1748 he was chosen to answer a petition executed against the town and received £13 6s. 8d. for his services at the General Court at Boston, and May 22, 1749, he was chosen " Representative of Berwick to the General Court at Boston, a selectman, and surveyor of lands. He was at the siege of Quebec, in 1754. He made his will September 10, 1756, which was proved the 13th of December following. He willed property to his wife Mercy, to children Moses, Thomas, Charles, James, John, Eliz-

abeth, Sarah, Mary, and Love Butler. He married
Mercy Wentworth, of Dover, N. H., and had

21. I. ELIZABETH,[3] baptized in South Berwick,
 September 2, 1727.
22. II. JOHN,[3] baptized with Elizabeth.
23. III. MOSES[3], baptized in South Berwick, February 1730/1.
24. IV. THOMAS,[3] baptized in South Berwick, May
 27, 1733.
25. V. CHARLES,[3] baptized in South Berwick, June
 8, 1735.
26. VI. MARTHA,[3] baptized in South Berwick, December 18, 1737.
27. VII. LOVE,[3] baptized in South Berwick, March
 30, 1740.
28. VIII. MARY,[3] baptized in South Berwick, May
 16, 1742.
29. IX. JAMES,[3] baptized in South Berwick, April
 26, 1747.
30. X. SARAH,[3] born in South Berwick.

7.

MARY,[3] first child of Thomas[2] and Mehitable Butler, was born in Berwick, and baptized July 17,
1726: married ——— Goodwin, and had WILLIAM[4]
GOODWIN (8) ; he is mentioned in his grandfather
Thomas' will, 1759 : she died before this time.

9.

OLIVE,[3] second child of Thomas[2] and Mehitable Butler, baptized March 31, 1728, married ———— Fippenny.

11.

ELIZABETH,[3] fourth child of Thomas[2] and Mehitable Butler, born in Berwick, and baptized September 12, 1731. Married ———— Sayward; was living in 1759.

12.

SAMUEL[3] BUTLER, fifth child of Thomas[2] and Mehitable, baptized May 19, 1734, and died July 15, 1799; married to Lydia, daughter of Nehemiah and Mary (Wentworth) Kimball, of Dover, N. H., May 4, 1757, by the Rev. Jeremy Belknap. Lydia died May 13, 1802. He inherited by his father's will two-thirds of the homestead where he lived and all his property in Quamphegan mills, besides other property. Mr. Butler was an extensive timber and lumber manufacturer and merchant. He was selectman of Berwick, and held other town offices. In 1772 he is recorded chosen " Moderator of town meeting." With others he signed a petition opposed to certain " oppressive and unconstitutional laws of the British Parliament for.

2

raising a revenue tax in North America." They had

31. I. ICHABOD,[4] born in South Berwick, July 4, 1758, baptized April 8, 1759.

32. II. SAMUEL,[4] born May 11, 1760, baptized August 31, 1760.

33. III. NEHEMIAH,[4] born July 29, 1762, baptized November 23, 1762.

34. IV. MEHITABLE,[4] born November 16, 1764, baptized November 25, 1764.

35. V. EPHRAIM,[4] born November 22, 1766, baptized December 14, 1766.

36. VI. LYDIA,[4] born February 3, 1768, baptized February 19, 1769.

37. VII. MARY,[4] born in South Berwick, July 25, 1771.

38. VIII. PELETIAH,[4] born in South Berwick, April 24, 1776.

39. IX. ROBERT,[4] born in South Berwick, July 11, 1778.

40. X. MARTHA,[4] born at South Berwick, March 16, 1780.

13.

MAJOR ICHABOD[3] BUTLER, sixth child of Thomas[2] and Mehitable Butler, baptized in Berwick, January 9, 1736/7; was a soldier in the war for independence.

14.

MOSES[3] BUTLER, seventh child of Thomas[2] and
Mehitable Butler, baptized in South Berwick, February 28, 1741/2, died September 21, 1823. He
married, December 18, 1764, Keziah Nason, died
July 28, 1824, and moved to the neighborhood
in Berwick known as Cranberry Meadows. At
the breaking out of the war for independence he
evinced a lively interest in the cause of the colonies, and was among the foremost in all measures
to promote the interests of freedom. He entered
the service with his brother, and served until its
close. There is no evidence that he was educated
to the law, although he acted in the capacity of
attorney for many years. In manner, though
genial, he was dignified, and was said by those
who knew him personally to have been one of the
most elegant gentlemen of his day. He was a
strict observer of the Sabbath, and seldom absent
from his seat in church on Sunday. Bountiful in
his charities, it was his custom, which he maintained as long as he lived, to invite to his table
all of the worthy poor of the parish on Christmas
and Thanksgiving Day, and if any were too feeble
or ill to be present on that occasion they were not
forgotten. He was one of the few in Maine who
owned slaves, and his kind treatment of them is
evinced as well by the fact that two of them re-
mained with him after emancipation as long as

he lived as by the testimony of his friends. He was fond of riding in the saddle, and at the age of eighty would mount his spirited horse from the ground without any aid. Their children were:

41. I. THOMAS,[4] born in Berwick, October 2, 1765.
42. II. MARY,[4] born in Berwick, January 15, 1767.
43. III. MOSES,[4] born in Berwick, June 22, 1769.
44. IV. WILLIAM G.[4], born in Berwick, May 3, 1771.
45. V. OLIVE,[4] born in Berwick, March 18, 1773.
46. VI. ICHABOD,[4] born in Berwick, August 22, 1775.
47. VII. BENJAMIN,[4] born in Berwick, August 14, 1777.
48. VIII. NATHAN,[4] born in Berwick, September 28, 1779.
49. IX. EDMOND,[4] born in Berwick, October 2, 1781; he died without issue.
50. X. JAMES,[4] born in Berwick, January 17, 1783.
51. XI. LOIS,[4] born in Berwick, April 2, 1786.

21.

ELIZABETH[3] BUTLER, first child of Captain Moses[2] and Mercy (Wentworth) Butler, who was baptized with her brother John, September 2, 1727; married, June 2, 1744, James Doughty.

22.

JOHN[3] BUTLER, second child of Captain Moses[2] and Mercy (Wentworth) Butler, baptized with

Elizabeth, September 2, 1727, married, March 15, 1761, Elisabeth Tucker, and had, with others,

52. I. JOHN,[4] baptized in Berwick, March 15, 1769.

23.

MOSES[3] BUTLER, third child of Captain Moses[2] and Mercy (Wentworth) Butler, baptized in Berwick, February, 1730/1, married, February 7, 1750, Sarah, daughter of Daniel and Abigail Goodwin. They were admitted communicants to the first church in South Berwick, January 26, 1752; had:

53. I. PETER,[4] baptized in South Berwick, March 8, 1752.

54. II. MARY,[4] baptized in South Berwick, February 24, 1754,

and perhaps others.

24.

THOMAS[3] BUTLER, fourth child of Captain Moses[2] and Mercy (Wentworth) Butler, baptized in Berwick, May 27, 1733. Was a soldier in the army of the Revolution. He was living in South Berwick in 1773, and signed a petition opposed to certain "laws of the British Parliament for raising a revenue tax in North America." Later in life he removed to Sanford, Me. He married, March 10, 1757, Bridget Gerrish, and had:

55. I. Moses,[4] baptized in Berwick, June 4, 1758.
56. II. William,[4] baptized with Moses; he died young.
57. III. Elizabeth,[4] baptized in Berwick, June 6, 1760.
58. IV. Nathaniel,[4] born July 5, 1761, baptized July 10, 1761.
59. V. Thomas,[4] baptized June 19, 1763.

These were all born in South Berwick:

60. VI. Mary.[4]
61. VII. Sarah.[4]
62. VIII. Eunice.[4]
63. IX. Hannah.[4]
64. X. Bridget.[4]
65. XI. Mercy.[4]
66. XII. Susan.[4]
67. XIII. William [4] again, born in Sanford, Me.

25.

CHARLES[3] BUTLER, fifth child of Captain Moses[2] and Mercy (Wentworth) Butler, baptized June 8, 1735. Was in the army of the Revolution. He was living in Salmon Falls, N. H., as late as 1773, was chosen constable June 18, 1764, and to various town offices afterward. He was a manufacturer of and trader in lumber, staves, etc. He signed a petition opposed to certain " laws of the British Parliament for raising a revenue tax in

North America." Later in life he moved to Sanford, Me., married Sally (Sarah) Cross, of Kittery,
Me.; had:

68. I. JOHN,[4] born in South Berwick; he was a
shipmaster; married in Boston, Mass., and died
at sea.

69. II. JOSEPH,[4] born in South Berwick, January
16, 1761.

70. III. BENJAMIN,[4] born in South Berwick; was a
shipmaster, and drowned November 1, 1789.

71. IV. MOSES,[4] born in South Berwick, January
21, 1766.

72. V. JAMES,[4] born in South Berwick.

73. VI. LOVE,[4] born in South Berwick.

74. VII. SARAH,[4] born in South Berwick, February
12, 1775.

75. VIII. NANCY,[4] born in South Berwick.

76. IX. ABIGAIL,[4] born in South Berwick, October
2, 1791.

27.

LOVE[3] BUTLER, seventh child of Capt. Moses[2]
and Mercy (Wentworth) Butler, was married
August 24, 1757, to James Percy, in South Berwick, by the Rev. Jacob Foster. They had:

77. I. STEPHEN[4] PERCY, baptized in South Berwick
November 19, 1758.

78. II. CHARLES[4] PERCY, baptized October 11, 1761.

79. III. JAMES[4] PERCY, baptized July 10, 1763.

These were all born in South Berwick.

29.

JAMES [3] BUTLER, ninth child of Capt. Moses [2] and Mercy (Wentworth) Butler, baptized in South Berwick, April 26, 1747; was living in Somersworth, N. H., in 1773, when he sold his share of a property in Salmon Falls of his late father, then occupied by his brother Charles; was married, November 22, 1769, to Elizabeth Hartford, in Dover, N. H., by the Rev. Jeremy Belknap; certificate granted in Berwick, November 18, 1769.

30.

SARAH [3] BUTLER, tenth child of Capt. Moses [2] and Mercy (Wentworth) Butler; was born in South Berwick; married William Nason, Jr.; had :

80. I. DORCAS [4] NASON, baptized in South Berwick, November 8, 1761.
81. II. LOIS [4] NASON, baptized in South Berwick, May 11, 1766.
82. III. WILLIAM [4] NASON.
83. IV. HANNAH [4] NASON.
84. V. JOSEPH [4] NASON.
85. VI. JAMES [4] NASON.
86. VII. ABRAHAM [4] NASON.

These five last named were all baptized in South Berwick, November 3, 1773.

31.

ICHABOD[4] BUTLER, first child of Samuel[3] and Lydia (Kimball) Butler, born July 4, 1758 ; married, December 20, 1786, Abigail, daughter of Colonel John and Abigail (Millet) Wentworth. She was born April 23, 1757, and died October, 1802. Wentworth says he was in the Revolutionary army and lived directly in front of what is known as Butler's Hill, in South Berwick, and died there September, 1810. It is likely that he inherited the homestead (as his father had done) and lived there. Old deeds describe him as a farmer, trader, and lumberman. He held various town offices, and was Town Clerk in 1801. Their children were :

87. I. JOHN WENTWORTH,[5] born in South Berwick, June 13, 1787 ; died at sea when about 18 years of age.

88. II. HARRIET,[5] born in South Berwick, April 15, 1789 ; died single, 1856.

89. III. ICHABOD,[5] born in South Berwick, June 30, 1791. He was a practising lawyer in Sanford, Me. He married, in 1823, Mary, daughter of Daniel Wise, Esq., of Kennebunk, Me., and widow of Moses Morrill. He died in Sanford, March 11, 1833. She died May, 1825. Their children were :

90. I. EDWARD HEYMAN,[6] died about a year after his mother.

91. II. Moses Morrill,[6] born in Sanford, March
8, 1824; he prepared for college at the academies of Alfred, Gorham, and North Yar-
mouth, and entered Bowdoin College in 1841,
where he graduated in the class of 1845 with
the highest honors. Immediately after graduating he was engaged for a time as teacher
of the High School in Springvale, at the
same time pursuing his studies for the profession of the law. Subsequently, he read
law with the Hon. E. E. Bourne, of Kennebunk, Me., and completed his course with the
Hon. Samuel Wells, of Portland, Me., subsequently one of the Judges of the Superior
Court of Maine. Mr. Butler was admitted to
the Cumberland County Bar, November 9,
1847, and immediately began practice in the
office in Portland vacated by the elevation of
his instructor, Mr. Wells, to the Bench. Shortly
after this he took the office of the Hon. Augustus
Haines, District Attorney of the United States.
He subsequently formed a law partnership with
the Hon. William Pitt Fessenden, which was
afterward continued with the sons of Mr. Fessenden. In December, 1875, he formed a partnership with Charles Libby, prosecuting attorney for Cumberland County, and afterward
Mayor of Portland. Mr. Butler was county attorney from 1859 to 1865, was twice Representative in the State Legislature, once in 1859,

and again at the time of his death. He was twice Mayor of Portland, Me., from 1877 to 1879, holding that office at the time of his death, and was chairman of the commission appointed to report on the condition of the Portland & Ogdensburg Railroad with reference to the city's interest therein. Mr. Butler was a careful and sagacious lawyer, with an eminently judicial mind. He ranked among the ablest jurists in the State. As Mayor of Portland his services (coming at a time when a lawyer of experience and sagacity was felt to be necessary) were believed to be particularly valuable, and gave unqualified satisfaction. The following short extract from the address of Judge Symonds in the Supreme Court upon the presentation of resolutions show his habits as a close student and industrious lawyer. "Mr. Butler was a man of great practical ability. He had the tastes and habits of a student, but the volume in his hand was usually a law-book. He was diligent in his reading, and kept pace with the works of the latest authors, and with the proceedings of the courts. In matters of recent interest and importance he was thoroughly equipped. He was a man of experienced and disciplined sagacity, a wise councillor, and prudent in the management of affairs." On October 9, 1879, while conducting a case in court, Mr. Butler suffered an attack of paralysis, and died on October 21, 1879. He married, in 1850, Olive M., only daughter of John M. Storer, Esq., of Sanford, Me. Their children were:

92. I. JOHN STORER,[7] born in Portland, died young.

93. II. HARRY,[7] born in Portland, February 22, 1858, graduated at Harvard College, in the class of 1879, and is Secretary of the Portland Trust Company.

94. III. GRACE,[7] born in Portland, March 4, 1876.

95. IV. GEORGE,[5] born in South Berwick, May 15, 1793; died at sea, leaving one child:

96. I. ESTHA A.[6] She married John Dean, of Paris, Me.

97. V. EDWARD HEYMAN,[5] born in South Berwick, July 1, 1800, died young.

32.

SAMUEL[4] BUTLER, second child of Samuel[3] and Lydia (Kimball) Butler, born in South Berwick, May 11, 1760, and died June 1, 1843; married, first, Susan Chadbourne. By this marriage there was no issue. By his second wife, Martha Libby, he had:

98. I. DANIEL,[5] born in South Berwick, April 1, 1784, died October 21, 1821; married, and had:

99. I. MARTHA,[6] who married Daniel Nason, and at least two others.*

* Wentworth.

100. II. MARY,[5] born in South Berwick, October 15, 1786, married Thomas Goodwin; no issue.

And by Nancy Shorey, his third wife, Samuel[4] had:

101. III. HIRAM,[5] born in South Berwick, December 26, 1789; married, December 1, 1813, Nancy, daughter of Timothy and Amy (Hodsdon) Wentworth. She was born April 29, 1791; died, April 27, 1870. He died August 13, 1867; they had:

102. I. SABINA,[6] born in South Berwick, May 20, 1814; married, December, 1842, James Robbins, lived in South Berwick, and had:

103. I. CHARLES[7] ROBBINS, born in South Berwick, May 8, 1846.

104. II. HARRIET A.[7] ROBBINS, born in South Berwick, August 30, 1849.

105. III. GEORGE H.[7] ROBBINS, born in South Berwick, October 28, 1859.

106. II. SHEPHERD N.,[6] born in South Berwick, September 28, 1817; married, August 10, 1845, Hulda Austin, of South Berwick. She was born May 7, 1821. They had:

107. I. NORRIS A.,[7] born in South Berwick, November 15, 1852; married, May 25, 1875, Christiana C. Wyman, of Rollinsford, N. H.; had:

108. I. J. B. G.,[8] born May, 1874.

109. II. ANNIE A.,[7] born in South Berwick, July 24, 1858; married, February 24, 1881, Frank R. Varney, of Rollinsford, N. H.; had:

110. I. ANNIE KATHARINE[8] VARNEY, born December 3, 1881.

111. II. JOHN SHEPHERD[8] VARNEY, born June 10, 1883.

112. III. HARVEY W.,[7] born in South Berwick, March 18, 1860.

113. III. THOMAS W.,[6] born in South Berwick, May 8, 1822; is single.

114. IV. LYDIA,[6] born in South Berwick, March 13, 1823; married, August 2, 1850, Joseph T. Chase, of Newburyport, Mass. He was born March 8, 1826, lived in Boston, and had:

115. I. JOSEPH T.[7] CHASE, born October 21, 1853.

116. II. LIZZIE E.[7] CHASE, born July 28, 1856.

117. III. HERBERT I.[7] CHASE, born June 27, 1858.

118. V. HIRAM A.[6] born in South Berwick, September 8, 1824; married, September 14, 1850, his cousin, Mary Wentworth, daughter of his mother's brother, Moses Wentworth. They had:

119. I. HERMAN WENTWORTH,[7] born in South Berwick, January 31, 1852.

120. II. JOHN FREDERICK,[7] born in South Berwick, February 14, 1857.

121. III. HIRAM ALONZO,[7] born in South Berwick, November 17, 1861.

122. VI. EMELINE C.,[6] born in South Berwick, April 2, 1827; married, March 18, 1862, William Burleigh, of South Berwick; lives in Wentworth, Mitchell County, Ia.; had, besides one who died in infancy:

123. I. Mary Elizabeth[7] Burleigh, born December 27, 1862.

124. VII. Harriet,[6] born in South Berwick, April 4, 1828.

125. IV. Oliver,[5] born in South Berwick, October 17, 1791; died January 1, 1868. He was Collector of Taxes in 1816; resided in Berwick, at Blackberry Hill, and married first, November, 1819, Abby Vickory Odiorne, of Portsmouth, N. H. She died March 4, 1855; married again, Mrs. Melinda Dorr. He had by first wife, besides one who died in infancy:

126. I. Haven Appleton,[6] born in Berwick, October 28, 1820; married, May 23, 1841, Lucy Perkins Ricker, of North Berwick; had:

127. I. J. Wesley,[7] born in North Berwick, died in 1847.

128. II. Charles Melville,[7] born in North Berwick, died in Washington, single, 1873.

129. III. John W.,[7] born in North Berwick, died in Penn., 1885; married, and has three children.

130. IV. Lucy Abby,[7] born in North Berwick, married, Fred. S. Hartwell, of Parsonsfield, Me.

131. V. Ella H.,[7] born in North Berwick; died young.

132. VI. Woodbury Haven,[7] born in North Berwick.

133. VII. Horatio Appleton,[7] born in North Berwick.

134. V. LYDIA,[5] born in South Berwick, November 17, 1793 ; died single.

135. VI. JOHN,[5] born December 11, 1795 ; died young.

136. VII. SABINA,[5] born December 21, 1797 ; died February 10, 1809.

137. VIII. JOHN[5] again, born in South Berwick, July 4, 1800, died 1832 ; married Widow Sarah M. Bartlett Morrill, of Elliott, Me.; had :

138. I. ELIZABETH,[6] born December 21, 1824 ; married, first, Daniel N. Perkins, of South Berwick ; second, John T. Young, of Strafford, N. H.; no issue.

139. II. CHARLES S.,[6] born March 20, 1827 ; married, first, Sarah Ricker, of Limerick, Me.; second, her sister, Elizabeth Ricker ; had :

140. I. SARAH A.,[7] born in South Berwick, married Charles Burleigh, of South Berwick.

141. II. CHARLES F.,[7] born in South Berwick.

142. III. NANCY S.,[6] born November 20, 1829 ; married, November 13, 1850, John Plummer, of South Berwick.

33.

NEHEMIAH [4] BUTLER, third child of Samuel [3] and Lydia (Kimball) Butler, was born in South Berwick, July 29, 1762, and died December 28, 1851. He married Mary Yeaton, of Portsmouth,

N. H. She was born June 11, 1763, and died April 11, 1853 ; had :

143. I. ANDREW,[5] born in South Berwick, October 28, 1787; died March 10, 1809, without issue.

144. II. WENTWORTH,[5] born in South Berwick, January 31, 1790 ; married Mehitable Tibbetts, February 25, 1817 ; she died January 24, 1818 ; he married again, September 13, 1823, Margaret Walsh.

145. III. NEHEMIAH KIMBALL,[5] born May 29, 1794, and married, August 26, 1819, Mary Green, of Portsmouth, N. H. She was born March 9, 1798. He moved to Augusta, Ga., and was a merchant there for many years ; had :

146. I. JOSEPH G.,[6] born in Portsmouth, N. H., June 20, 1820, and died September 24, 1820.

147. II. CHARLES G.,[6] born in Augusta, Ga., September 23, 1821 ; married, August 14, 1864, Elizabeth A. Tipton, of Barnwell, S. C., had :

148. I. KIMBALL,[7] born February 10, 1866, died February 26, 1867.

149. II. CHARLES C.,[7] born March 29, 1867, died June 14, 1869.

150. III. ROBERT E. L.,[7] born in South Carolina, June 5, 1869.

151. IV. MARY E.,[7] born in South Carolina, January 23, 1871.

152. V. BUDD,[7] born March 7, 1873, died April 5, 1873.

153. III. Sarah Ann Elizabeth,[6] born in Augusta, Ga., November 5, 1823; married, April 29, 1841, John Mulford Clark. They had :

154. I. Amos Kimball[7] Clark, born in Edgefield, S. C., August 21, 1842, and married, June 7, 1866, Elizabeth W. Freeman ; had :

155. I. Ann Elizabeth[8] Clark, born June 1, 1867, died December 10, 1871.

156. II. Clifford Ware[8] Clark, born December 3, 1868, died December 8, 1871.

157. III. Marion Amos[8] Clark, born March 4, 1871.

158. IV. Nellie Maud[8] Clark, born September 11, 1872.

159. V. Lulu Alice[8] Clark, born July 10, 1874.

160. II. John W.[7] Clark, born in Edgefield, S. C., April 26, 1844, married, April 15, 1869, Emma Thursby, of Kentucky.

161. III. Anna C.[7] Clark, born in Edgefield, S. C., April 9, 1846, married, December 17, 1872, D. Franklin Jack; had :

162. I. Effie C.[8] Jack, born October 15, 1873.

163. II. Frank[8] Jack, born February 11, 1875.

164. IV. Charles Perchard[7] Clark, born July 24, 1848.

165. V. Job A. A. W.[7] Clark, born September 5, 1850, married, August 31, 1870, Hattie Fargoe; had :

166. I. Joseph Clinton[8] Clark, born May 22, 1871.

167. II. HERBERT WINANS[8] CLARK, born August 8, 1873.

168. III. CARRY AUGUSTA BARRY[8] CLARK, born December 19, 1876.

169. VI. FRANCIS RALPH[7] CLARK, born February 24, 1853 ; is a graduate of the University of Georgia.

170. VII. CHARLES EDGAR[7] CLARK, born in Augusta, Ga., January 14, 1855.

171. VIII. ALICE GERTRUDE[7] CLARK, born in Augusta, Ga., November 1, 1860.

172. IV. CAROLINE AUGUSTA,[6] born in Augusta, Ga., January 19, 1826, died July 11, 1870 ; married, August 18, 1841, J. M. C. Freeland, of Edgefield, S. C.; had :

173. I. SANFORD EUGENE[7] FREELAND, born in Edgefield, S. C., August 2, 1842 ; married, February 18, 1860, Mary Parkman ; had :

174. I. IDA AUGUSTA[8] FREELAND, born in Edgefield, S. C., December 30, 1860.

175. II. WILLIAM E.[8] FREELAND, born April 10, 1862.

176. III. JOSEPH F.[8] FREELAND, born (twin with William E.[8]) April 10, 1862.

177. IV. MAGGIE ANN L.[8] FREELAND, born January 3, 1864.

178. V. EDNA DORA[8] FREELAND, born March 24, 1866.

179. VI. ROBERT F.[8] FREELAND, born September 19, 1867.

180. VII. JAMES M.⁸ FREELAND, born (twin with Robert F.) September 19, 1867.

181. VIII. MAMIE LEE⁸ FREELAND, born in Edgefield, May 4, 1870.

182. IX. CHARLES YOUNG⁸ FREELAND, born in Edgefield, September 9, 1871.

183. II. MARY FRANCES⁷ FREELAND, born September 24, 1844, married, November 14, 1867, Leroy J. Miller.

184. III. JAMES PLEASANT⁷ FREELAND, born December 25, 1845 ; married, March 12, 1868, Caroline A. Willis ; had :

185. I. WILLIS EUGENE⁸ FREELAND, born February 20, 1870.

186. II. SUSAN AUGUSTA⁸ FREELAND, born September 6, 1871.

187. III. MARY FRANCES⁸ FREELAND, born March 20, 1874.

188. IV. WALTER RANDOLPH⁸ FREELAND, born May 10, 1876.

189. IV. GERTRUDE A.⁷ FREELAND, born March 8, 1848, married, December 25, 1873, John D. Bentley.

190. V. CHARLES HENRY⁷ FREELAND, born November 25, 1849, married, February 10, 1875, Josephine Payne ; had :

191. I. CAROLINE A.⁸ FREELAND, born February 15, 1876.

192. II. JULIA C.⁸ FREELAND, born July 9, 1878.

193. VI. JULIA CLAYTON⁷ FREELAND, born January

9, 1852, married, February 6, 1868, P. P. Wilhirt; had :

194. I. KIMBALL ALBERT[8] WILHIRT, born June 4, 1869.

195. II. HERBERT[8] WILHIRT, born June 8, 1871.

196. III. MARY D.[8] WILHIRT, born August 30, 1874.

197. IV. JUNIUS EARL[8] WILHIRT, born February 6, 1877.

198. VII. WILLIAM[7] FREELAND, born March 25, 1854; died October 15, 1854.

199. VIII. WALTER BUTLER[7] FREELAND, born September 29, 1855.

200. IX. CARRIE WING[7] FREELAND, born January 6, 1858.

201. X. NEHEMIAH K.[7] FREELAND, born March 4, 1860 ; died November 11, 1862.

202. XI. EMMA C.[7] FREELAND, born October 11, 1862.

203. XII. EDGAR H.[7] FREELAND, born March 12, 1865.

204. XIII. LEROY M.[7] FREELAND, born March 7, 1870.

205. V. MARY FRANCES,[6] born in Augusta, Ga., February 17, 1828 ; married, October 3, 1848, Richard S. Key, of Augusta, Ga.; had :

206. I. SARAH E.[7] KEY, born July 20, 1849 ; married, January 24, 1867, John Ewen Holmes ; had :

207. I. MINNIE C.[8] HOLMES, born in Augusta, January 29, 1868.

208. II. John S.[8] Holmes, born in Augusta, Ga., July 10, 1870.

209. III. Kate Lee [8] Holmes, born in Augusta, April 8, 1873.

210. IV. Patience M.[8] Holmes, born in Augusta, Ga., April 30, 1876.

211. II. Marcellus O.[7] Key, born September 20, 1851, died May 5, 1865.

212. III. Cara O.[7] Key, born December 30, 1853 ; died July 5, 1855.

213. IV. Julia A.[7] Key, born in Augusta, Ga., April 25, 1856.

214. V. Charles H.[7] Key, born in Augusta, December 12, 1862.

215. VI. Richard C. B.[7] Key, born August 12, 1866.

216. VI. Julia E.,[6] born April 18, 1830 ; married, January 3, 1854, Ralph P. Clark; had :

217. I. James W.[7] Clark, born May 5, 1855; died in infancy.

218. II. Joseph W.[7] Clark, born January 23, 1857 ; died June 13, 1857.

219. III. William David [7] Clark, born May 3, 1859.

220. IV. Mary E.[7] Clark, born August 22, 1861.

221. V. Kate L.[7] Clark, born June 19, 1863.

222. VI. Ralph P.[7] Clark, born March 26, 1868 ; died February 25, 1871.

223. VII. Ralph Butler [7] Clark, born January 21, 1876.

224. VII. Catharine C.,[6] born in Augusta, January 17, 1833 ; married, December 3, 1850, Henry F. Freeman; had :

225. I. Henrietta[7] Freeman, born September 10, 1851.

226. VIII. Nehemiah K.,[6] born in Augusta, Ga., January 29, 1835 ; married, November 24, 1858, Anna Latham, of Augusta ; no issue.

227. IX. John Samuel,[6] born September 26, 1837 ; died November 9, 1838.

228. X. John William,[6] born October 8, 1840 ; died June 18, 1841.

229. IV. Phineas,[5] born February 14, 1792 ; died August 1, 1858. He moved to Augusta, Ga., in 1820, and was for many years a merchant there ; married, August 17, 1823, Harriet Wooster, of Berwick, Me. ; had :

230. I. Amanda M.,[6] born in Augusta, Ga., August 8, 1825 ; died March 10, 1873 ; married, September 30, 1841, Willey B. Griffin ; had five sons and five daughters.

231. II. Harriet A.,[6] born in Berwick, Me., August 17, 1827 ; died July 23, 1828.

232. III. Georgiana L.,[6] born in Augusta, Ga., May 2, 1829 ; died February 28, 1866 ; married, June 9, 1855, Charles W. Bond ; had one son and one daughter.

233. IV. Harriet A.,[6] born in Augusta, Ga., March 19, 1831 ; died February 28, 1869 ; married,

August 13, 1848, William B. Smith, of Augusta, Ga.; had five children.

234. V.   MARK W.,[6] born in Augusta, May 16, 1833; died October 5, 1844.

235. VI.   JOSEPHINE D.,[6] born in Augusta, April 29, 1836; died December 27, 1868; married, June 20, 1852, William H. Philpot; had three sons and five daughters.

236. VII.   JANE M.,[6] born in Augusta, Ga., July 10, 1838; married, May 5, 1858, Asbury F. Smith; had one son,

237. I.   ASBURY[7] SMITH.

238. VIII.   PHINEAS,[6] born July 28, 1840; died June 5, 1841.

239. IX.   MINERVA A.,[6] born March 29, 1842; died March 26, 1868; married, June 5, 1859, Richard G. Dennott; had two daughters.

240. X.   GEORGE P.,[6] born in Augusta, Ga., March 19, 1845. He was cashier of the Georgia R. R. Bank; married M. E. Horague of Augusta; had one son and one daughter.

241. V.   MEHITABLE,[5] born in Berwick, Me., May 29, 1797; married, December 29, 1819, Phineas Pray; had one child, who died young. She died August 9, 1820.

242. VI.   MARY,[5] born in Berwick, Me., June 9, 1799; married Prentis Pealer; had:

243. I.   JOHN[6] PEALER, born in Berwick; died young.

244. II.   CHARLES[6] PEALER, born in Berwick; died young.

245. III. MARY [6] PEALER, born in Berwick ; married Albert N. Dennison ; they had :

246. I. ARTHUR [7] DENNISON, born in Berwick, February 22, 1859.

247. II. IDA [7] DENNISON, born in Berwick, February 22, 1861.

248. III. ALICE [7] DENNISON, born in Berwick, May, 1863.

249. IV. GEORGE [7] DENNISON, born in Berwick, July 9, 1866.

250 V. MARY [7] DENNISON, born in Berwick, February 22, 1873.

251. VI. GRAY [7] DENNISON, born in Berwick, February, 1876.

252. VII. DORCAS,[5] born October 24, 1801 ; died August 13, 1821.

253. VIII. SAMUEL,[5] born in Berwick, June 24, 1804; died July 12, 1870 ; married Sarah Hanson, of Berwick ; had :

254. I. ALBERT,[6] born in Berwick, April 8, 1831 : married MARY E. BROWN ; died December 12, 1859, without issue.

255. II. MARY,[6] born in Berwick, September 30, 1832; married Joseph Brown, of Berwick; had :

256. I. GEORGE A.[7] BROWN, born in North Berwick, May 15, 1862.

257. II. CHARLES [7] BROWN, born in North Berwick, December 19, 1864.

258. III. SAMUEL BUTLER [7] BROWN, born in North Berwick, September 1, 1871.

259. IV. Daniel[7] Brown, born in North Berwick, January 20, 1873.

260. III. Phineas,[6] born in Berwick, July 5, 1834 ; married Esther Hibbs, and died without issue, September, 1864.

261. IV. Susan,[6] born in Berwick, July 16, 1836 ; married Uriah Blaisdell; had :

262. I. Idalia Alice [7] Blaisdell, born in Great Falls, N. H., April, 1863.

263. II. Susan Butler[7] Blaisdell, born in Great Falls, N. H., 1868.

264. V. Daniel H.,[6] born in Berwick, September 24, 1838.

265. VI. William N.,[6] born in Berwick, October 14, 1840; married, 1866, to Lydia E.[7] (381), daughter of Nathaniel[5] (361) and Lydia (Bean) Butler, by the Rev. S. L. Holman, pastor of the Baptist church of Berwick; had:

266. I. Carrie E.,[7] born in Berwick, February 2, 1867.

267. II. William N.,[7] jr., born in Berwick, February 24, 1869.

268. III. Grace E.,[7] born in Berwick, May 28, 1870.

269. IV. Albert N.,[7] born in Berwick, August 2, 1873.

270. V. Florence M.,[7] born in Berwick, February 14, 1876.

271. VII. Samuel Kimball,[6] born in Berwick, March 24, 1843.

272. VIII. MELINDA,[6] born in Berwick, August 6, 1845 ; married, January 8, 1873, Frank Wallingford.

273. IX. SARAH E.,[6] born in Berwick, January 2, 1850.

274. X. ANDREW J.,[6] born in Berwick, June 28, 1852.

275. XI. CHARLES W.,[6] born in Berwick, July 28, 1855.

276. IX. NANCY,[5] born in Berwick, January 22, 1807 ; married John M. Hanson ; had :

277. I. PHINEAS [6] HANSON, born in Berwick, May 18, 1827. He was a trader in South Carolina ; married Miss Hobbs, of North Berwick, and died without issue.

278. II. THADDEUS [6] HANSON, born in Berwick, November 15, 1828 ; is married, and lives in Berwick.

279. III. LYDIA [6] HANSON, born in Berwick.

280. IV. AMANDA [6] HANSON, born in Berwick; married ; has no issue.

281. V. HARRIET [6] HANSON, born in Berwick.

282. VI. MARY [6] HANSON, born in Berwick; married David Webber.

283. VII. JOHN [6] HANSON ; died young.

284. X. MELINDA,[5] born in Berwick, February 25, 1811; married James Hanson, of North Berwick; died without issue.

35.

EPHRAIM [4] BUTLER, fifth child of Samuel [3] and
Lydia (Kimball) Butler, born November 26, 1766;
married Lydia Libby; had:

285. I. EPHRAIM K.,[5] born in South Berwick, March
21, 1793; married Lydia Horn, of Lebanon,
Me.; had:

286. I. JOHN HORN,[6] born in South Berwick, September 18, 1819; married Elizabeth B. Pool, of
Boston, Mass.; had:

287. I. EMMA R.,[7] born in South Berwick, April 10,
1848, late Postmistress of Salmon Falls, N. H.

288. II. LEWIS,[6] born in South Berwick; married
Mrs. Priscilla Shackford; is living in Moultonborough, N. H.; has one child, Lulu.

289. III. SYLVESTER,[6] born in South Berwick; un-
married.

290. II. SAMUEL,[5] born in South Berwick, May 21,
1796, married Abigail Butler, of Tamworth,
N. H.; had one daughter, now a widow in
Moultonborough.

291. III. FREDERICK,[5] born in South Berwick, May
17, 1799; died March 28, 1802.

292. IV. ESTHER,[5] born in South Berwick, January
4, 1811; died 1815.

37.

MARY[4] BUTLER, seventh child of Samuel[3] and
Lydia (Kimball) Butler, born July 25, 1771; married Thomas Goodwin, of South Berwick; had:

293. I. FANNY[5] GOODWIN, born in South Berwick,
about 1798; married, 1834, Alexander Stowell;
had:

294. I. MARY[6] STOWELL, born in South Berwick,
1836; married, about 1856, Frank Pike; had:

295. I. ETTA H.[7] PIKE.

296. II. GERTRUDE[7] PIKE.

297. II. ABEL[6] STOWELL, born about 1840; married
Rose Pope; had:

298. I. CARRIE[7] STOWELL.

299. II. MARY[7] STOWELL.

300. III. FANNIE[7] STOWELL.

301. IV. JOHN[7] STOWELL.

302. V. FRED[7] STOWELL.

303. II. MARY[5] GOODWIN, born in South Berwick
about 1800; married Andrew Reynolds; had:

304. I. SAMUEL[6] REYNOLDS; married Lizzie Mills;
had:

305. I. LIZZIE[7] REYNOLDS.

306. II. FRANK[7] REYNOLDS.

307. III. LOUISA[7] REYNOLDS.

308. IV. MARY ANN[7] REYNOLDS.

309. V. ANDREW[7] REYNOLDS.

310. III. ELIZA[5] GOODWIN, born in South Berwick,

January 8, 1802 ; married, October 26, 1823, Daniel Andrews, born April 12, 1801 : had :

311. I. George W.[6] Andrews, born February 13, 1824; married, November 16, 1848, Hannah[5] Butler (1065), daughter of James[4] and Hannah (Grant) Butler ; had :

312. I. George[7] Andrews, born in Berwick, August 16, 1850.

313. II. Hannah[7] Andrews, born October 10, 1852 ; both died in infancy. He married again, July 12, 1857, Elizabeth Jane Hall ; had :

314. III. Etta Cora[7] Andrews, born August 13, 1858.

315. IV. Frank Elmer[7] Andrews, born April 11, 1861; married Mamie Hurd.

316. V. George Albert[7] Andrews, born May 30, 1863.

317. VI. Emma Catherine[7] Andrews, born August 12, 1864.

318. VII. Eliza Ann[7] Andrews, born April 19, 1866.

319. VIII. Mary Belle[7] Andrews, born September 23, 1867.

320. II. Rev. Thomas J.[6] Andrews, born February 12, 1826. He was a Baptist divine; married Harriet Eaton ; died without issue.

321. III. Mary E.[6] Andrews, born October 1, 1827; married, December 12, 1848, Moses W.[5] Butler (1066), son of James[4] and Hannah (Grant) Butler, whom see for children.

322. IV. JAMES W.[6] ANDREWS, born May 8, 1829; married, June 8, 1861, Caroline Hill; had:

323. I. LAURA I.[7] Andrews, born July 25, 1862.

324. II. JAMES W.[7] ANDREWS, born September 15, 1864.

325. III. MARY E.[7] ANDREWS, born March 13, 1867.

326. IV. SARAH J.[7] ANDREWS, born October 24, 1868.

327. V. CLARK HILL[7] ANDREWS, born October 20, 1872.

328. VI. CHARLES EVERETT[7] ANDREWS, born March 28, 1875.

329. VII. HERBERT T.[7] ANDREWS, born April 14, 1876.

330. V. EDMUND G.[6] ANDREWS, born April 10, 1832; married, March 12, 1857, Mary Seavey; had:

331. I. AURELIA F.[7] ANDREWS, born August 23, 1859; married, in 1880, Charles Andrews.

332. II. THOMAS G.[7] ANDREWS, born May 2, 1861.

333. III. DANIEL BUTLER[7] ANDREWS, born December 12, 1863.

334. IV. MARY S.[7] ANDREWS, born July 18, 1871; Edmund married again in 1879, Vinnie Gibson.

335. VI. ANDREW J.[6] ANDREWS, born September 15, 1833; married, February 2, 1855, Sarah Seavey; had:

336. I. GEORGE WASHINGTON[7] ANDREWS, born June 18, 1857.

337. II. CHARLES FREDERICK [7] ANDREWS, born February 19, 1869.

338. III. NELLIE E. [7] ANDREWS, born July 23, 1874.

339. VII. DANIEL G. [6] ANDREWS, born in Berwick, January 29, 1835; is now a resident of Concord, N. H.   He has served as Representative of Concord in the State Legislature, and as a member of the Governor's Council; married, in 1869, Maria Tucker.

340. VIII. WILLIAM B. [6] ANDREWS, born January 15, 1837; married, December 15, 1868, Miranda Wakefield; had:

341. I. HERBERT W. [7] ANDREWS, born March 23, 1870.

342. II. CARRIE BELLE [7] ANDREWS, born November 4, 1871.

343. III. MARY ELIZA [7] ANDREWS, born October 31, 1873.

344. IV. LYDIA [5] GOODWIN, born about 1803; married George Jackson; had:

345. I. SARAH A. [6] JACKSON.

346. II. CHARLES T. [6] JACKSON; married Kate Smith, about 1858; had:

347. I. FRED H. [7] JACKSON, born about 1860.

348. II. MARY E. [7] JACKSON.

349. III. LYDIA M. [6] JACKSON, born 1840; married L. G. Swett; had:

350. I. G. JACKSON [7] SWETT, born 1874.

351. V. SAMUEL [5] GOODWIN, born 1805; married Hannah Williams; had:

352. I. SARAH⁶ GOODWIN, born in 1834; married Rev. J. M. Bailey; had:
353. I. EDDIE⁷ BAILEY, born 1868.
354. II. CHARLES⁷ BAILEY.
355. III. GRACE⁷ BAILEY.
356. VI. SABINA⁵ GOODWIN, born 1807; married Edmund Griffiths; had:
357. I. MARY E.⁶ GRIFFITHS, born 1834.
358. II. EDMUND⁶ GRIFFITHS, born 1838.
359. VII. SARAH A.⁵ GOODWIN; married Edmund Griffiths, husband of her elder sister, Sabina, in 1842.
360. VIII. ALBERT T.⁵ GOODWIN.

38.

PELETIAH⁴ (Paltiah?) BUTLER, eighth child of Samuel³ and Lydia (Kimball) Butler, born in South Berwick, April 24, 1776; married Betsy Goodwin, 1799. She was born August 21, 1777; had:
361. I. NATHANIEL,⁵ born in South Berwick, October 17, 1799; married, December, 1828, Lydia Bean, of Sanford, Me.; born September 28, 1796; had:
362. I. SARAH ELIZABETH,⁶ born in Berwick, January 14, 1831; married Moses Jellison, and had:
363. I. ANGELINE⁷ JELLISON, born in South Berwick.

4

364. II. George[7] Jellison, born in South Berwick.

365. III. Mary[7] Jellison, born in South Berwick.

366. IV. John[7] Jellison, born in South Berwick.

367. V. Martin[7] Jellison, born in South Berwick.

368. VI. Annette[7] Jellison, born in South Berwick.

369. VII. Elvira[7] Jellison, born in South Berwick.

370. II. Eliza A.,[6] born in South Berwick, June 7, 1833; married John Thurrill; had:

371. I. Nathaniel[7] Thurrill, born in South Berwick, November 17, 1867.

372. II. Nellie[7] Thurrill, born in South Berwick, September 21, 1870.

373. III. Delia[7] Thurrill, born in South Berwick, July 31, 1875.

374. IV. John W.[7] Thurrill, born in South Berwick, July 20, 1877.

375. III. Lucy H.,[6] born in South Berwick, June 5, 1835; married Richard L. Goodwin; had:

376. I. Cora B.[7] Goodwin, born June 4, 1864; died an infant.

377. II. Charles[7] R. Goodwin, born in Berwick, June 26, 1866.

378. III. Albert H.[7] Goodwin, born in Berwick, April 7, 1868; died in infancy.

379. IV. Alice L.[7] Goodwin, born in Berwick, August 27, 1870; died young.

380. IV. MARY OLIVE,[6] born July 12, 1837; died young.

381. V. LYDIA E.,[6] born in South Berwick, April 24, 1840; married William N.[6] Butler (265), son of Samuel[5] (253) and Sarah (Hanson) Butler, whom see for children.

382. VI. OLIVE,[6] born in South Berwick; died young.

383. VII. ELLA,[6] born in South Berwick; died young.

384. II. OLIVE,[5] born in South Berwick, July 12, 1801; married Ebenezer Thompson; 2. Hiram Keay; had, by first husband:

385. I. WILLIAM H.[6] THOMPSON, born February 9, 1824; married Louisa[5] (994), daughter of Nathan[4] (48) and Adah (Chick) Butler, whom see for children.

386. III. MARY,[5] born in South Berwick, May 16, 1804; married Isaac Smith; had:

387. I. HARRIET[6] SMITH, born in South Berwick.

388. II. ELMIRA[6] SMITH, born in South Berwick.

389. III. GEORGE[6] SMITH, born in South Berwick.

390. IV. BARTLETT[6] SMITH, born in South Berwick.

391. V. MARY O.[6] SMITH, born in South Berwick.

392. VI. LYDIA[6] SMITH; died young.

393. VII. NICHOLAS[6] SMITH; died young.

394. VIII. NATHAN[6] SMITH.

395. IX. RUSHA[6] SMITH.

396. X. LYDIA[6] SMITH again.

397. IV. SALLY,[5] born in South Berwick, August

10 (30 ?), 1806; married Benjamin Gilpatrick; had :

398. I. John H.[6] Gilpatrick, born in South Berwick.

399. II. Sarah[6] Gilpatrick, born in South Berwick.

400. III. Luella[6] Gilpatrick, married Ivory Clark

401. V. John,[5] born May 11, 1809 ; married, January 9, 1839, Mary Warren, born April 9, 1813 ; had :

402. I. Harriet,[6] born July 12, 1840; married Charles Moses; had :

403. I. John E.[7] Moses, born November, 1870.

404. II. Charles O.[7] Moses, born September 3, 1872.

405. III. Kate W.[7] Moses, born February, 1878.

406. II. Mary,[6] born April 20, 1842.

407. III. Abbie,[6] born in South Berwick.

408. IV. John H.,[6] born May 10, 1847.

409. V. William M.,[6] born March 29, 1849.

410. VI. Henry,[5] born in South Berwick, December 12, 1811 ; died young.

411. VII. George W.,[5] born September 3, 1814 ; married, September 17, 1848, Martha Gowell ; had seven children ; all but two died young, viz. :

412. I. Boyilla,[6] born in South Berwick.

413. II. Mary J.[6]

414. VIII. Harriet,[5] born May 22, 1819 ; died September 17, 1821.

39.

ROBERT[4] BUTLER, ninth child of Samuel[3] and Lydia (Kimball) Butler, born July 11, 1778 ; died January, 1855 ; married Sarah Drew; she died August 3, 1851 ; had :

415. I. LYDIA KIMBALL,[5] born in South Berwick, September 16, 1808 ; married, January, 1843, Ephraim K. Brock, of Dover, N. H.; she died July, 1881 ; had :

416. I. MARTHA K.[6] BROCK, born in Dover, N. H., December, 1833.

417. II. BENJAMIN FRANKLIN,[5] born in South Berwick, May 10, 1810 ; married, January[8], 1833, Mary Tilton; is a merchant in Boston ; they had :

418. I. HORACE BLAGDON,[6] born in Portsmouth, N. H., November 26, 1833; married Sarah A. Hamilton ; had :

419. I. LYMAN HAMILTON,[7] born September 5, 1857.

420. II. BERTHA FLORENCE,[7] born November 19, 1860.

421. III. BLANCHE EVELYN,[7] born May 11, 1873.

422. IV. HATTIE BELLE,[7] born April 28, 1876 ; died September 16, 1883.

423. V. MARY E. GRIFFITH,[7] born June 15, 1879.

424. II. GEORGE AUGUSTUS,[6] born in Boston, January 15, 1836 ; married, first, Sarah E. Thomas ; second, Lucy Sawyer ; had :

425. I. LILLIAN,[7] born June 22, 1861; married Joseph Whipple: died July 8, 1883.

426. II. KATE,[7] born January 24, 1872.

427. III. GEORGIA ELLA.[7]

428. IV. GEORGE A.[7]

429. V. HENRY T.[7]

430. III. EDWARD PAYSON,[6] born in Boston, March 8, 1838; married Martha G. McMullin; had:

431. I. FRANK EUGENE,[7] born October 8, 1861.

432. II. JOHN EDWARD,[7] born June 29, 1863.

433. III. MARY,[7] born January 7, 1866.

434. IV. SARAH TILTON,[6] born in Boston, August 6, 1840; married W. H. H. Emmons; had:

435. I. HARRY BUTLER[7] EMMONS, born July 29, 1867.

436. II. GRACE[7] EMMONS, born March 5, 1869.

437. III. JENNY[7] EMMONS, born July 13, 1871.

438. IV. EDITH[7] EMMONS, born January 6, 1878; died March 3, 1883.

439. V. PAUL DYER[7] EMMONS, born April 25, 1884.

440. V. BENJAMIN FRANKLIN,[6] born in Boston, February 14, 1844; married Louisa A. Odiorne; had:

441. I. PERCY WALBACK,[7] born August 4, 1872; died August 8, 1873.

442. II. HERBERT FRANKLIN,[7] born March 2, 1875.

443. III. HAROLD ODIORNE,[7] born March 16, 1876.

444. IV. NELLIE LOUISE,[7] born July 3, 1879.

445. VI. MARY JANE,[6] born in Boston, October 10, 1846; married Henry Newcomb; had:

446. I. ELMIRA[7] NEWCOMB, born July 12, 1874.

447. VII. ELIZABETH FREEMAN,[6] born in Boston, July 7, 1849; is single.

448. III. AUGUSTUS,[5] born in South Berwick, May 20, 1812. He is a merchant in New York, lives in Brooklyn, N. Y.; married, September 29, 1835, Sarah A. Campbell, of Brooklyn, N. Y.; had:

449. I. EMILY A.,[6] born in Brooklyn, N. Y., August 10, 1836; married, May 19, 1859, George A. Newman; had:

450. I. GEORGE WALLACE[7] NEWMAN, born in Brooklyn, December 8, 1862; died April 8, 1866.

451. II. EMILY GRACE[7] NEWMAN, born October 23, 1864; married, October 1?, 1884, Alonzo D. Kittle; had:

452. I. GEORGE OAKLEY[8] KITTLE, born July 30, 1885.

453. II. JOSEPH H.,[6] born in Brooklyn, September 19, 1838; married, June 14, 1865, Sarah Davenport, of New Canaan, Conn.; had:

454. I. WINIFRED D.,[7] born in Brooklyn, April 6, 1866.

455. II. RENA,[7] born November, 1868; died May, 1871.

456. III. SAMUEL C.,[7] born in New Canaan, Conn., October 8, 1872.

457. IV. SARAH,[7] born in New Canaan, 1877; died September 29, 1882.

458. III. AUGUSTUS F.,[6] born in Brooklyn, July 3,

1840 ; married, March 7, 1878, Linda F. Baby ; no issue.

459.   IV. Dorcas E.[6], born in Taunton, Mass., August 21, 1846 ; married, July 11, 1865, Dr. William Henry Randolph ; no issue.

460.   V. Lydia M.,[6] born in Brooklyn, July 8, 1849 ; married, December 11, 1872, Henry E. Tuthill, of Brooklyn ; had :

461.   I. Henry R.[7] Tuthill, born in Brooklyn, November 22, 1873.

462.   II. Louis Butler[7] Tuthill, born in Brooklyn, August 27, 1875 ; died March 26, 1882.

463.   III. Gertrude M.[7] Tuthill, born in Brooklyn, May 25, 1878.

464.   IV. Henry Tuck,[5] born in Somersworth, N. H., December, 1814.   He was for some years an iron manufacturer in Taunton, Mass. ; died in California ; married Caroline Cheever ; no issue.

465.   V. Hannah,[5] born in Somersworth, N. H., December, 1816 ; single.

466.   VI. William R.,[5] born in Somersworth, N. H., June 20, 1820 ; lived in New York, where he died single, November, 1874.

467.   VII. John Q. A.,[5] born in South Berwick, Me., September 14, 1824 ; is a commission merchant in New York ; married, in Lowell, Mass., May 18, 1848, Almira E. Wood, of Blue Hill, Me.   She was born June 15, 1824 ; had :

468. I. WILLIAM M.,[6] born in Lawrence, Mass., June 14, 1849 ; died July 14, 1849.

469. II. ROBERT,[6] born in Brooklyn, N. Y., October 23, 1851; is a merchant in New York. He married Ella M. Raynor. She was born September 23, 1851 ; had :

470. I. JOHN Q. A.,[7] born in Brooklyn, May 3, 1874.

471. II. ROBERT N.,[7] born January 12, 1876.

472. III. CHARLES RAYNOR,[7] born April 21, 1878.

473. IV. AUGUSTUS H.,[7] born August 22, 1880.

474. V. ENOCH F.,[7] born November 6, 1882.

475. III. HENRY,[6] born in Brooklyn, February 20, 1853; died May 9, 1853.

476. IV. THOMAS SOUTHARD,[6] born April 24, 1854 ; died May 26, 1862.

477. V. HANNAH M.,[6] born in Mount Vernon, N.Y., October 13, 1856 ; died October 26, 1856.

478. VI. A daughter born in Mount Vernon, August 9, 1859 ; died September 12, 1859.

479. VII. JOHN HENRY,[6] born in Brooklyn, November 9, 1861 ; died August 9, 1862.

41.

THOMAS[4] BUTLER, first child of Moses[3] and Keziah (Nason), born October 2, 1765; baptized November 24, 1765 ; married Dorcas Hodsdon ; moved to Lebanon. He was a justice for many years, and was at one time the unsuccessful candi-

date of his party for Representative in Congress.
He left no issue. He married a second time,
August 27, 1835, Thankful Dixon.

42.

MARY[4] BUTLER, second child of Moses[3] and
Keziah (Nason) Butler, born in Berwick, June
15, 1767; married, October 11, 1788, Ebenezer
Ricker, of Lebanon, Me.; had:

480. I. Moses[5] Ricker, born in Lebanon, Me., January 20, 1790; died December 17, 1873;
married Keziah Hodsdon, of Berwick; had:

481. I. Edmund[6] Ricker, born October 29, 1809;
married, January 17, 1837, Theodosia Grant, of
Acton, Me.; had:

482. I. Henry[7] Ricker, born April 23, 1841; married Nancy J. Shapleigh, of Lebanon Centre,
Me.; had:

483. I. George H.[8] Ricker, born July 23, 1865;
died December 14, 1868.

484. II. Edward E.[8] Ricker, born March 11, 1868.

485. III. Eliza J.[8] Ricker, born March 15, 1870.

486. IV. George H.[8] Ricker, born January 4, 1874.

487. V. Lavonia G.[8] Ricker, born August 15, 1875.

488. VI. Ina E.[8] Ricker, born August 18, 1876.

489. VII. Angeline E.[8] Ricker, born November
26, 1878.

490. II. Amy[6] Ricker, born March 5, 1812; no
issue.

491. III. EZEKIEL⁶ RICKER, born February 26, 1814;
died December 1, 1877; married, December 12,
1836, Hannah Wentworth, of Lebanon, Me.;
had:

492. I. JAMES A.⁷ RICKER, born July 19, 1838; died
February 5, 1870; married, February 15, 1860,
Juliet Ricker, of Sanford, Me.; had:

493. I. FLORA⁸ RICKER, born September 3, 1861.

494. II. LINWOOD D.⁸ RICKER, born December 25,
1863; died December 2, 1867.

495. II. ANN A.⁷ RICKER, born March 14, 1840; is
single.

496. III. NANCY J.⁷ RICKER, born February 23,
1847; died October 20, 1880; married, April
26, 1873, Humphrey Grant, of Lebanon.

497. IV. WILLIAM⁶ RICKER, born May 8, 1816; is
single.

498. V. EBENEZEᴀ⁶ RICKER, born September 9,
1818; married, March 1, 1843, Louisa Grant,
of Acton, Me.; had:

499. I. MOSES⁷ RICKER, born in Acton, December
20, 1843; married, November 1, 1868, Harriet
B. Wentworth, of Eastport, Me.

500. II. CHARLES H.⁷ RICKER, born May 13, 1846;
married, April 26, 1877, Hannah Cloutman, of
Acton, Me.

501. III. MARY F.⁷ RICKER, born November 25,
1851; married, March 25, 1874, Horace E.
Sanborn, of Acton, Me.; died January 4,
1880.

502. VI. George Hodgdon[6] Ricker, A.M. (Professor), born in Lebanon, Me., December 23, 1820. He was prepared for college under the private tuition of Rev. James Weston, and at the Parsonsfield Seminary. During this time he taught various district schools, beginning at the early age of sixteen years. He graduated from Dartmouth College in 1845. Soon after graduating he became principal of the Parsonsfield Seminary, in which position he continued seven years. He was afterward professor of the Greek and Latin languages, a few years, in Whitestown Seminary, N. Y. From this institution he went to Lewiston, Me., to fill a similar position in Bates College. More recently he was professor of the Greek language and literature in Hillsdale College, Mich. He is the author of a series of English grammars. He married, December 2, 1847, Harriet Newell, daughter of Mark A. and Huldah (Neal) Chase, of Newfield, Me.; had:

503. I. Harriet Georgiana[7] Ricker, born January 21, 1857. She is a teacher of French and Latin in the Melrose High School, Mass.

504. VII. Mary[6] Ricker, born May 11, 1823; died August 19, 1867; married, July 5, 1846, Gershom Jones, of Lebanon, Me.; had:

505. I. Nancy J.[7] Jones, born November 9, 1847; married Richard Horn.

506. II. Annie[7] Jones, born December 19, 1850;

married Francis A. Shapleigh, of Lebanon Centre, Me.

507. VIII. URANIA[6] RICKER, born April 29, 1825; married, October 19, 1848, Seaver Jones, of Lebanon, Me.; had:

508. I. HELEN U.[7] JONES, born May 3, 1854; died April 15, 1856.

509. II. HELEN U.[7] JONES, born July 3, 1857; died June 12, 1863.

510 IX. ASA H.[6] RICKER, born September 1, 1827; died September 19, 1877; married, December 18, 1850, Jane Jones; had:

511. I. ALVIN H.[7] RICKER, born July 1, 1855; married, May 30, 1876, Fannie Knox, of Lebanon, Me.; had:

512. I. ASA J.[8] RICKER, born February 8, 1880.

513. X. ANGELINA[6] RICKER, born February 10, 1830; died January 1, 1847.

514. XI. MIRANDA J.[6] RICKER, born May 5, 1834; died November 5, 1858.

515. II. OLIVE[5] RICKER, born December 10, 1793; died December 3, 1871; married, November 24, 1814, Nicholas Staples, of Tamworth, N. H.; he was born June 30, 1790; died January 12, 1849. They had:

516. I. CATHARINE[6] STAPLES, born May 18, 1817; married, October 2, 1842. Judge Larkin D. Mason, of Tamworth, N. H. He was born in Tamworth, May 16, 1810; was chosen Representative in the New Hampshire Legislature

in 1852–53. Was Senator in 1855. Again Representative in 1860. Was appointed military agent for the State of New Hampshire in 1862, which office he held until 1866. He was appointed Judge of Probate for the County of Carroll in 1864, and held this office (excepting a few months) until 1880, when his term expired by limitation (at the age of seventy), according to the Constitution of the State. Judge Mason was at one time Prohibition candidate for Governor of New Hampshire. They had:

517. I. CLINTON S.[7] MASON, born in Tamworth, N. H., October 28, 1843. He is a successful merchant in Boone, Boone County, Ia.; married, May 7, 1872, Annetta Noyes; had:

518. I. ARTHUR L.[8] MASON, born in Tilton, N. H., October 15, 1873.

519. II. HOWARD CURRY[8] MASON, born in Boone, Ia., September 3, 1875.

520. III. FRANCIS BELL[8] MASON, born in Boone, Ia., June 26, 1877.

521. IV. CATHARINE S.[8] MASON, born in Boone, Ia., November 2, 1879.

522. II. JOANNA F.[7] MASON, born in Tamworth, October 13, 1844; died August 14, 1878; married, at Georgetown, January 25, 1864, Edward L. Larrebee; had:

523. I. FRANK D.[8] LARREBEE, born July 15, 1865.

524. II. JOHN E.[8] LARREBEE, born November 24, 1866.

525. III. KATIE MAUD [8] LARREBEE, born December 28, 1868.

526. IV. JOSIE MABEL [8] LARREBEE, born January 16, 1877.

527. III. CHARLES T. T.[7] MASON, born in Tamworth, May 31, 1846 ; is a resident of Boone, Boone County, Ia.

528. IV. NICHOLAS W.[7] MASON, born in Tamworth, November 20, 1847. He is a merchant in North Sandwich, N. H.; married, April 3, 1879, Emma Dame ; had :

529. I. LUTIE EMMA [8] MASON, born in North Sandwich, February 12, 1880.

530. V. SARAH OLIVE [7] MASON, born May 7, 1849 ; died March 4, 1850.

531. VI. JOHN L.[7] MASON, born in Sandwich, November 24, 1850. He is a merchant ; married, at Rochester, N. H., June 15, 1876, Nellie Varney ; had :

532. I. NELLIE ADELAIDE [8] MASON, born October 18, 1879.

533. VII. SARAH OLIVE [7] MASON, born in Sandwich, September 4, 1852.

534. VIII. MARY ELIZABETH [7] MASON, born in Sandwich, October 5, 1855.

535. IX. JUSTINE E.[7] MASON, born in Sandwich, July 13, 1858.

536. X. HENRY M.[7] MASON, born in Sandwich, December 7, 1859.

537. II. OLIVE [6] STAPLES, born November 30, 1819;

married, November 25, 1840, Josiah Bean, of Tamworth, N. H.; had :

538. I. Helen M.[7] Bean, born September 5, 1841.

539. II. George F.[7] Bean, born August 30, 1845.

540. III. Daniel O.[7] Bean, born March 31, 1847; died July 12, 1850.

541. III. David [6] Staples, born February 15, 1822; died February 21, 1822.

542. IV. Susan R.[6] Staples, born October 19, 1823; married, March 10, 1844, Charles P. Cook, of Tamworth, N. H.; he has represented Tamworth in the State Legislature, and is now first Selectman of the town; had :

543. I. Clinton [7] Cook.

544. V. David R. C.[6] Staples, born December 2, 1827; died May 5, 1832.

545. III. Mary [5] Ricker, born September 7, 1795; died September 10, 1870; married, May 23, 1814, Thomas Ricker, of Lebanon; had :

546. I. Elvira [6] Ricker, born August 29, 1815; died January 6, 1850; married, October 20, 1844, John G.[5] Butler (1058), son of James [4] (50) and Hannah (Grant) Butler.

547. II. Eliza [6] Ricker, born May 24, 1818; married, August 17, 1845, George Guptill, of Berwick, Me.; had :

548. I. Martha A.[7] Guptill, born January 18, 1846; married, July 15, 1868, Charles Plummer, of Great Falls, N. H.; had :

549. I. Oswald [8] Plummer, born April 5, 1870.

550. II. Joseph [7] Guptill, born March 18, 1847.

551. III. Alice [7] Guptill, born June 2, 1848.

552. IV. Jennie [7] Guptill, born May 13, 1850.

553. V. Thomas R. [7] Guptill, born June 3, 1854; died May 13, 1856.

554. VI. Linnie F. [7] Guptill, born December 13, 1856.

555. VII. Sadie E. [7] Guptill, born May 1, 1858; married, November 30, 1876, Frank Thompson; had:

556. I. Harold B. [8] Thompson, born May 4, 1878.

557. III. Lewis C. [6] Ricker, born November 12, 1820; married Harriet E. Turner, of Boston, Mass.; had:

558. I. L. Edgar [7] Ricker, born July 15, 1849.

559. IV. William A. [6] Ricker, born December 26, 1822; married, August 17, 1844, Betsey Jones, of Lebanon, Me.; had:

560. I. Cyrus [7] Ricker, born October 17, 1845.

561. II. Emily [7] Ricker, born December 12, 1846.

562. III. William E. [7] Ricker, born July 6, 1848.

563. IV. Susan E. [7] Ricker, born August 12, 1853.

564. V. Sewell F. [7] Ricker, born May 17, 1855.

565. V. Thomas [6] Ricker, Jr., born August 14, 1825; married Elizabeth F. Fernald, of Lebanon, Me.; had:

566. I. Luella [7] Ricker, born February 21, 1858; married J. S. P. Jones.

567. II. Alta [7] B. Ricker, born April 3, 1864.

5

568. VI. Cyrus⁶ Ricker, born December 2, 1830; died May 30, 1840.

569. VII. Clinton⁶ Ricker, born August 10, 1832; died February 24, 1868; married Sarah Guptill, of Lebanon; had:

570. I. Clinton⁷ A. Ricker, born August 17, 1856.

571. VIII. Isaac N.⁶ Ricker, born August 9, 1839.

572. IX. Mary Ellen⁶ Ricker, born April 27, 1842.

573. IV. Dorcas⁵ Ricker, born December 9, 1799; died June 27, 1869; married Benjamin Hayes, of Lebanon; born November 1, 1798; died February 16, 1860; had:

574. I. Andrew⁶ Hayes, born January 14, 1819; married January 3, 1842, Caroline Gowell; born May 22, 1818; had:

575. I. Mary O.⁷ Hayes, born December 18, 1842; died July 18, 1844.

576. II. Olive M.⁷ Hayes, born May 12, 1844; married, December 5, 1862, Nathaniel D. Jones, of Lebanon; had:

577. I. Stephen A.⁸ Jones, born May 29, 1864.

578. II. Carrie M.⁸ Jones, born January 9, 1866.

579. III. Nathaniel S.⁸ Jones, born January 27, 1871.

580. IV. Erdix S.⁸ Jones, born with Nathaniel S., January 27, 1871.

581. V. Harold B.⁸ Jones, born February 24, 1882.

582. VI. Ethel W.⁸ Jones, born August 3, 1884.

583. III. Winfield S.⁷ Hayes, born December 17,

1846; married, January 1, 1880; Katie Lang, of Baltimore, Md.

584. IV. Sarah M.[7] Hayes, born March 29, 1852; married January 1, 1870; William H. Tasker, of Charlestown, Mass.; had:

585. I. Clarence E.[8] Tasker, born October 9, 1872.

586. II. Andrew L.[8] Tasker, born March 11, 1874.

587. III. Blanche M.[8] Tasker, born May 26, 1884; died January 1, 1885.

588. IV. Ralph H.[8] Tasker, born February 9, 1885.

589. V. Nellie F.[7] Hayes, born April 4, 1854; married, November 27, 1881, Thomas Baker, of East Boston, Mass.; had:

590. I. Leslie M.[8] Baker, born October 13, 1882.

591. VI. Andrew W.[7] Hayes, born August 9, 1857; married, October, 1880, Harriet Lincoln, of Quincy, Mass.; had:

592. I. Gertrude L.[8] Hayes, born October, 1882; died October, 1884.

593. II. Ethel [8] Hayes, born July, 1885.

594. VII. James F.[7] Hayes, born April 5, 1859.

595. VIII. Henry L.[7] Hayes, born May 3, 1861; died August 29, 1875.

596. II. Ebenezer R.[6] Hayes, born December 19, 1821; died April 15, 1854.

597. III. Sarah [6] Hayes, born May 23, 1823; died September 25, 1837.

598. IV. James [6] Hayes, born April 8, 1828; died September 17, 1837.

599. V. Charles F. [6] Hayes, born September 29, 1831; died August 16, 1838.

600. VI. Mary [6] Hayes, born May 13, 1834; died January 6, 1841.

601. V. Ebenezer [5] Ricker, born September 9, 1803; died December 2, 1841; married August 26, 1826, Susan G. [5] Butler (773), of Sandwich, N. H., daughter of William G. [4] (44) and Abigail Butler, born October 23, 1802; died September 12, 1877; had:

602. I. John B. [6] Ricker, born May 25, 1828; married December 15, 1848, Experience Wentworth, of Lebanon, Me.; had:

603. I. Carrie B. [7] Ricker, born September 29, 1857; married, John Bunford, of Somersworth, N. H.; had:

604. I. Minnie B. [8] Bunford, born July 16, 1877.

605. II. Rose D. [8] Bunford, born October 22, 1883.

606. II. Clinton S. [6] Ricker, born October 25, 1831; married, January 1, 1858, Adeline [6] (726) Butler, of Milton Mills, N. H.; had:

607. I. Ida S. [7] Ricker, born March 24, 1859; married, September 17, 1880, James W. Merrow, of Milton, N. H.

608. III. Chapman S. [6] Ricker, born April 3, 1834; died October 20, 1878; married, December 12,

1857, Martha A. Richardson, of Medfield,
Mass.; had:

609. I. ABBIE⁷ RICKER, born September 13, 1858;
married Perley Wright, of Westford, Mass.

610. II. CARRIE A.⁷ RICKER, born at Medfield, March
4, 1860.

611. III. CORA F.⁷ RICKER, born April 15, 1861;
died October 5, 1861.

612. IV. MARY J.⁷ RICKER, born in Medfield, October 7, 1863.

613. V. GEORGE E.⁷ RICKER, born May 3, 1867.

614. IV. MARY⁶ RICKER, born April 10, 1837; married, May 16, 1863, Enoch P. Sherman, of Lebanon, Me.; had:

615. I. CARLOS W.⁷ SHERMAN, born December 12,
1869.

616. II. JOHN L.⁷ SHERMAN, born March 10, 1872.

617. III. JENNIE M.⁷ SHERMAN, born August 17,
1876.

618. V. ABBIE⁶ RICKER, born February 20, 1839;
married John F.⁶ Butler (1545), of Springvale,
Me., son of John B.⁵ and Lucinda (Heard) Butler and grandson of Moses⁴ (71) and Abigail
(Pugsley) Butler, whom see for children.

43.

MOSES⁴ BUTLER, third child of Moses³ and
Keziah (Nason) Butler, born in Berwick, June
22, 1769; was a trader in Lebanon, Me. He

married Dorcas Ricker, of Berwick. Wentworth says this "Dorcas had property given her by will (dated April 20, 1795) of her father Moses Ricker, son of Maturin, Jr., and grandson of Maturin Ricker the emigrant." They had:

619. I. Dorcas,[5] born in Lebanon, February 13, 1793; married Benjamin Knox (whose first wife was her younger sister Keziah). She had:

620. I. Keziah[6] Knox, born March 19, 1825; married Charles Coolidge, of Brookline, Mass., August 7, 1846; had:

621. I. Sarah[7] Coolidge, born July 27, 1847; married, December 24, 1868, Calvin Rice; had:

622. I. Louis W.[8] Rice, born October 26, 1872.

623. II. Mabel[8] Rice, died young.

624. II. Annie F.[7] Coolidge, born May 25, 1851; is a teacher and singer.

625. III. Susan[7] Coolidge, born September 8, 1858; married, February 1, 1883, Liman E. Wait.

626. II. Caroline[6] Knox, born April 1, 1827; is single.

627. II. Keziah,[5] born March 12, 1795; married, November 6, 1819, Benjamin Knox; had:

628. I. Moses[6] Knox, born May 19, 1821; died May 20, 1853; married Lydia Wiggin; had one child, died in infancy.

629. III. Lucy,[5] born May 5, 1797; died May 15, 1861; married Jacob Hersom, certificate granted July 31, 1819; had:

630. I. Louisa [6] Hersom, born September 19, 1821; married Payson Libby, of Lebanon, Me., and died November 10, 1851.

631. II. Mary Ann [6] Hersom, born August 31, 1823; married, April 28, 1843, Eli Jones, of Lebanon, Me.; had:

632. I. Louisa A. [7] Jones, born November 6, 1852; died March 7, 1862.

633. II. Jacob E. [7] Jones, born July 4, 1857; married, February 29, 1880, Flora Murray, of Lebanon; had:

634. I. Ralph J. [8] Jones, born March 15, 1883.

635. III. Harriet [6] Hersom, born March 17, 1826; died March 31, 1855; married Joseph Goodwin, of Lebanon; had:

636. I. Harriet E. [7] Goodwin, born July 1, 1854; married, first, April 12, 1877, Charles Lord, of Sanford; again, May 1, 1883, Edward Grant, of Lebanon; had:

637. I. Charles [8] Grant, born April 29, 1884.

638. II. Ernest [8] Grant, born April 18, 1885.

639. II. Martha [7] Goodwin, born with Harriet [7] E., July 1, 1854.

640. IV. Moses R., [5] born in Lebanon, July 16, 1799; died 1857; married Nancy Stevens, of Shapleigh, published October 19, 1822; had:

641. I. John S., [6] born in Lebanon, September 22, 1823. He was educated at the Academies of Parsonsfield, Me., and Durham, N. H. On leaving the Durham Academy he taught the

public schools of his native town, and in the
town of Lee, N. H.   He has taught in a private
school in Utah for some time, and later, in
1853, a public school near Salt Lake City.
On December 16, 1849, Mr. Butler took pas-
sage on a sailing vessel which left Boston Har-
bor, and arrived in San Francisco, July 9, 1849,
by way of the Straits of Magellan. He has
engaged in mining, stock raising, and prospect-
ing at different times since then, and is now,
since 1870, living in Kernville, Kern County,
Cal. He is fond of books and the company of
literary men.   He married, May 1, 1872, Mary
Elizabeth Caldwell, of Louisiana, Mo.

642. II. DORCAS,[6] born in Lebanon, March 25, 1825;
married Hiram H. Goodwin, January 1, 1850;
had:

643. I. HARRIET S.[7] GOODWIN, born November 21,
1850; married, September 7, 1873, Lewis B.
Weeks, of Parsonsfield, Me. ; had:

644. I. HIRAM E.[8] WEEKS, born September 14, 1876.

645. II. LILLIAN EDNA[8] WEEKS, born December 20,
1878.

646. III. LEWIS ERNEST[8] WEEKS, born September
11, 1880.

647. IV. ARTHUR LEON[8] WEEKS, born October 20,
1882.

648. V. EDITH V.[8] WEEKS, born December 17,
1883.

649. II. CLARA E.[7] GOODWIN, born May 19, 1854;

married, March 10, 1876, Melvin Wentworth, of Lebanon ; had :

650. I. LILLIAN M.[8] WENTWORTH, born January 1, 1878.

651. II. WINIFRED[8] WENTWORTH, born February 19, 1880.

652. III. JOSEPHINE[8] WENTWORTH, born April 6, 1881.

653. IV. CARRIE[8] WENTWORTH, born January 2, 1884.

654. V. BESSIE[8] WENTWORTH, born October 13, 1885.

655. III. LIZZIE[7] GOODWIN, born February 4, 1862 ; married, July 2, 1885, Alvah Tibbitts.

656. III. FERNALD,[6] born in Lebanon, May 13, 1828. He is a timber manufacturer and merchant in Thomasville, Ga. During the war of the rebellion he served in the Confederate army as commissary. He married Maryland Adams, born August 3, 1843 ; had :

657. I. ANNIE,[7] born September 22, 1862.

658. II. GEORGIA,[7] born November 16, 1863 ; died January 16, 1864.

659. III. TOMMINETTE,[7] born May 26, 1865.

660. IV. LYDIA HARLOW,[7] born September 8, 1867.

661. V. MARYLAND,[7] born July 4, 1869 ; died August 11, 1872.

662. VI. MOSES R.,[7] born January 29, 1871.

663. VII. FERNALD H.,[7] born August 25, 1873.

664. VIII. JOHN,[7] born February 13, 1878.

665. IX. HARRIS,[7] born September 13, 1880; died September 17, 1880.

666. X. AARON,[7] born September 5, 1883.

667. IV. MAJOR H. MOSES,[6] born in Lebanon, February 14, 1831. He is a builder in Georgia. During the war of the rebellion he was a major in the Confederate army.

668. V. ALVAH,[6] born in Lebanon, January 5, 1833; married, November 22, 1857, Lydia A. Harlow, of Braintree, Mass.; had:

669. I. SARAH,[7] born August 24, 1875.

670. VI. SUSAN,[6] born in Lebanon, December 16, 1840; married, January, 1870, John M. Hays, of Lebanon; had:

671. I. JENNIE[7] HAYS.

672. II. LIZZIE[7] HAYS.

673. V. MARY,[5] born in Lebanon, May 11, 1804; died September 19, 1882; married, October 16, 1825, James Pray, born in Lebanon, March 5, 1799; had:

674. I. WILLIAM MARCUS[6] PRAY, born April 3, 1826; married, June 17, 1848, Elizabeth[6] (1504), daughter of David and Sarah[5] (1503) (Butler) Marsh, of Springvale, Me. Lives in Boston, Mass.; for children see descendants of Sarah[5] Butler and David Marsh.

675. II. DR. MARK W.[6] PRAY, born in Lebanon, now living in Malden, Mass., and is a dentist in Boston; married, October 22, 1851, Jane M. Bartlett, of Charlestown, Mass.; had:

676. I. GEORGE B.[7] PRAY, born March 5, 1853; died November 8, 1861.

677. II. JOSEPHINE A.[7] PRAY, born October 10, 1856; married Marshall S. Rice, November 9, 1881; had:

678. I. ARTHUR PRAY[8] RICE, born September 22, 1882.

679. II. Son born November 8, 1885.

680. III. NELLIE M.[7] PRAY, born January 14, 1859; died January 30, 1863.

681. IV. GEORGIANA[7] PRAY, born June 7, 1864.

682. V. WILLIAM MARK[7] PRAY, born October 3, 1866.

683. III. MARY[6] PRAY, born in Lebanon, January 18, 1833; married, 1861, Job Harris, a merchant in Berwick, Me., and died without issue about 1870.

684. IV. LUCY A.[6] PRAY, born in Lebanon, December 28, 1834; married, October 2, 1854, Nelson Stanley, of Boston, Mass.

685. V. SARAH[6] PRAY, born in Lebanon, January 16, 1837; married, August 3, 1880, Rev. D. H. Stoddard, of Great Falls, N. H.

686. VI. JAMES E. S.[6] PRAY, born in Lebanon, July 30, 1843; married, March, 1861, Nellie A. Young, of Great Falls, N. H. She died in 1882, and he married again, September 29, 1883, Mary E. Morrison, of Exeter, N. H.

687. VI. WILLIAM,[5] born in Lebanon, September 8, 1807; married, January 23, 1830, Mary A. Goodwin; had:

688. I. EDWARD,[6] born May 21, 1831; died June 9,

1872; married, in Roxbury, Mass , October 9, 1853, Ann Mullins, born in Ireland, May 24, 1829; had:

689. I. WILLIAM,[7] born in Melrose, Mass., July 12, 1854. Lives in North San Juan, Cal.

690. II. CHARLES E.,[7] born in Melrose, Mass., May 30, 1857; died April 19, 1859.

691. III. MARY JANE,[7] born in Melrose, Mass., April 21, 1859; married Seldon W. Long, 1873, of Fryeburg, Me.; had:

692. I. VELORUS[8] LONG, born in North San Juan, January 27, 1874.

693. II. EMMA[8] LONG, born April 12, 1875.

694. III. FLORA[8] LONG, born in San Juan, August 8, 1876.

695. IV. IDA[8] LONG, born in Cherokee, October 8, 1878.

696. V. MELVIN[8] LONG, born in Cherokee, November 2, 1879.

697. VI. FREDDIE[8] LONG, born June 24, 1881.

698. VII. MOLLIE[8] LONG, born August 8, 1883; died September 19, 1883.

699. IV. ANNIE,[7] born in San Francisco, Cal., March 1, 1864.

700. V. EDWARD,[7] born in Pike City, Cal., September 27, 1867; died January 11, 1869.

701. VI. JOHN H.,[7] born in North San Juan, Cal., November 5, 1871.

702. II. OLIVER,[6] born in Lebanon, September 13, 1832; died 1833.

703. III. Melissa,[6] born February 25, 1854; married, first, July 4, 1865, Charles Bowley, of Exeter, N. H.; second, George C. Eaton; had:

704. I. Fannie[7] Bowley, born in Exeter, September 4, 1866.

705. II. Lizzie[7] Eaton, born July 31, 1874.

706. IV. Sarah,[6] born February 5, 1836; married, March 20, 1867, Gershom Jones; had:

707. I. Susan,[7] Jones, born January 28, 1872.

708. II. Luther[7] Jones, born August 6, 1876.

709. V. Francis,[6] born October 31, 1838; died July 21, 1866; married, Martha Jones; had:

710. I. Fannie[7] married Joseph Curtis; had:

711. I. William F.[8] Curtis.

712. VI. William F.,[6] born September 20, 1840; married Harriet Prescott; had:

713. I. Effie,[7] born May 14, 1867.

714. VII. Mary E.,[6] born June 7, 1843; married Lorenzo D. Goodwin; had:

715. I. Almeda[7] Goodwin, born September 13, 1865.

716. II. Loring[7] Goodwin, born May 14, 1867.

717. III. Fanny[7] Goodwin, born July 2, 1869.

718. IV. William L.[7] Goodwin, born September 23, 1872.

719. V. Christiana B.[7] Goodwin, born April 19, 1876.

720. VI. Mary A.[7] Goodwin, born December 2, 1882.

721. VIII. Olive A.,[6] born June 11, 1845; married George A. Pugsley; had:

722. I. WILLIAM[7] PUGSLEY, born September 10, 1876.

723. II. JOHN B.[7] PUGSLEY, born November 21, 1882.

724. IX. JOHN S.,[6] born August 1, 1849; died single, January 1, 1882.

725. VII. THOMAS,[5] born in Lebanon, December 16, 1809; married, August 21, 1831, Hannah Lord; had:

726. I. ADELINE,[6] born January 18, 1833; died November 12, 1880; married, December 26, 1857, Clinton S.[6] Ricker (606), of Lebanon; had:

727. I. IDA S.[7] RICKER, born in Lebanon, March 24, 1859; married, September 17, 1879, James W. Merrow.

728. II. WENTWORTH,[6] born 1835; died 1864.

729. III. HANNAH A.,[6] born March 3, 1838; married Millet Roberts, of Milton; had:

730. I. FRANK L.[7] ROBERTS, born February 26, 1860; married, April 15, 1884, Grace Tibbetts, of Great Falls, N. H.; had one son, born December 8, 1885.

731. II. FANNIE[7] ROBERTS, born with Frank L.,[7] February 26, 1860.

732. III. HANNAH[7] ROBERTS, born May 1, 1862.

733. IV. WENTWORTH M.[7] ROBERTS, born June 19, 1866; died May 17, 1868.

734. V. WENTWORTH S.[7] ROBERTS, born April 10, 1869.

735. VI. JAMES E.[7] ROBERTS, born March 19, 1874.

736. VII. BESSIE M.[7] ROBERTS, born February 17, 1884.

737. IV. MALVESTER,[6] born August 15, 1842; married, February 10, 1868, Frank H. Chesley; had:

738. I. ARTHUR A.[7] CHESLEY, born September 25, 1870.

739. II. ROWLAND E.[7] CHESLEY, born July 24, 1882.

740. V. ORESTA A.,[6] born December 22, 1847.

44.

WILLIAM G.[4] BUTLER, fourth child of Moses[3] and Keziah (Nason) Butler, born in Berwick, Me., May 5, 1771; baptized May 19, 1771; married Abigail Cross, of Portsmouth, N. H. He lived in Standish, Me.; had:

741. I. WILLIAM E.,[5] born in Standish, August 5, 1793; married May 27, 1817, Hannah Paine, of Standish. She was born February 17, 1792; had:

742. I. WILLIAM PAINE,[6] born in Standish, May 23, 1818; married Christine Jamison, in Wilkesbarre, Pa., August 5, 1843. Lived for a time in Wisconsin, but now resides in Manchester, N. J.; had:

743. I. FRANK OSRO,[7] born in Wilkesbarre, Pa., 1849; married, had:

744. I. William P.,[8] died young.

745. II. Lucy M.,[7] born in Wisconsin, May 27, 1856; died young.

746. III. Nellie G.,[7] born May 17, 1867. And four others who died young.

747. II. John H.,[6] born in Thomaston, Me., October 11, 1819. He is a lawyer in Boston, Mass. He graduated at the Fryeburg Academy in 1842, and was one of the Committee of Arrangements for its Centennial celebration. Mr. Butler graduated at Harvard College in the class of 1846, taking a high rank in his class of sixty members. He was elected the same year sub-master in the Brimmer School of Boston; and, three years later, was chosen master in the same school. He served in the latter capacity three years. During this time he studied law, and in 1852 commenced the practice of law, a member of the Suffolk Bar, in Boston. Although Mr. Butler has served as a member of various nominating committees he has never accepted political office. He is an active member of his church, and has been superintendent of its Sabbath-school for more than fourteen years. He has lived an active life, his practice being in the higher courts of the commonwealth. He married, in 1849, Charlotte P. Libby, of Portland, Me.; had:

748. I. Elliot Libby,[7] born in Boston, May 9, 1852; married Ida M., daughter of Washington and

Margaret Belt. She was born May 15, 1862. He is a merchant in New York, and resides in Jersey City, N. J.

749. II. EMMA B.,[7] born in Boston, March 18, 1856.

750. III. GEORGE W.,[6] born in Standish, N. H., January 25, 1822; married, December 31, 1846, Sarah L. Mitchell; had:

751. I. HERBERT L.,[7] born in Portland, June 7, 1847.

752. II. GEORGIA,[7] born in Portland, October 9, 1850.

753. III. DELIA,[7] born in Hallowell, Me., December 25, 1854.

754. IV. JOSEPH RICH,[6] born in Standish, January 25, 1825; married, February, 1852, Sophronia Baxter Spare, of Boston. She died April 2, 1856; he married again Fannie Bugbee. He had, by first wife, Sophronia Baxter Spare:

755. I. ELLA S.,[7] born February 9, 1856; married Percy M. Lauterman, in Chicago, Ill. By second wife he had:

756. II. WILLIAM LINCOLN,[7] born in 1865.

757. III. EUGENE,[7] born in 1867.

758. IV. FLORA,[7] born in 1874.

759. V. CHARLES,[6] born in Standish, November 29, 1830. He is a leather merchant in Boston, Mass.; married, December 19, 1860, Sarah M. Freeman. She died December 30, 1861; married again, May 24, 1877, Harriet Lang, of Boston, Mass.

6

760. VI. Lucy W.,[6] born in Standish, Me., August 27, 1832. She was an assistant teacher in the Brimmer School in Boston with her brother John H.;[6] is single.

761. VII. Frank,[6] born in Bethlehem, N. H., December 26, 1834; died August 20, 1862.

762. II. Ivory,[5] born in Standish, Me., December 3, 1794; married, May 11, 1817, Sarah Shaw. He received a grant of land in Lawn Ridge, Ill., to which he removed in 1846, and where he died, about 1870; they had:

763. I. Ivory C.,[6] born in Lebanon, Me., 1818; died in Chicago, Ill.

764. II. Salome.[6]

765. III. Sarah Ann,[6] married Levi Butler, and died in Methuen, Mass., about 1874, without issue.

766. IV. Sylvester,[6] died in the war of the rebellion.

767. V. Augusta,[6] born in Burlington, Vt.; married ——— Marsh.

768. III. Thomas Cass,[5] born in Standish, Me., March 6, 1796; he was for some years Collector of Customs for the United States at Derbyline, Vt.; married Phœbe Ann Baldwin in Stanstead, Canada; had:

769. I. Dennison,[6] born at Derbyline, Vt.

770. IV. John C.,[5] born in Standish, February 7, 1798; died December, 1817.

771. V. Abigail C.,[5] born in Standish, October 19,

1800; died February 3, 1831; married Samuel[5] Butler (290), of Moultonborough, N. H., March 1, 1825; had:

772. I. ABIGAIL,[6] born February 3, 1831; married —— Earl; he died in the war of the rebellion.

773. VI. SUSAN G.,[5] born in Standish, October 23, 1802; died September, 1877; married Ebenezer[5] Ricker (601), of Lebanon, Me.; had:

774. I. JOHN[6] RICKER, born in Lebanon.

775. II. CLINTON S.[6] RICKER, born in Lebanon, October 25, 1831; married, January 1, 1858, Adeline[6] Butler (726), daughter of Thomas[5] (725) and Hannah (Lord) Butler, of Milton Mills, N. H.; had:

776. I. IDA S.[7] RICKER, born in Lebanon.

777. III. CHAPMAN S.[6] RICKER, born in Lebanon.

778. IV. MARY[6] RICKER, born in Lebanon. (See descendants of Ebenezer Ricker and Susan G.[5] (601).)

779. VII. MOSES,[5] born in Standish, June 30, 1805; married, June 18, 1832, Grace B. Vittum, in Sandwich, N. H. She was born in Sandwich, December 12, 1808; had:

780. I. PHEBE ANN,[6] born May 12, 1834.

781. II. LUCY GRACE,[6] born March 15, 1836; married, October 17, 1863, Samuel Batchelder; had:

782. I. JESSIE GRACE[7] BATCHELDER, born in Salem, N. H., October 1, 1864.

783. III. Susan Ricker,[6] born August 29, 1838; died September 13, 1839.

784. IV. Daniel Coss,[6] born May 8, 1840; died December 11, 1877.

785. V. Susan Abbie,[6] born December 21, 1842.

786. VIII. Mary Ann,[5] born in Standish, Me., February 1, 1810.

45.

OLIVE[4] BUTLER, fifth child of Moses[3] and Keziah (Nason) Butler; born in Berwick, March 18, 1773; married, April 1, 1796, Joseph Hersom; had:

787. I. Joseph[5] Hersom, born August 15, 1798; died January 20, 1862; married, February 15, 1827, Betsy Lord, of Lebanon; had:

788. I. Lydia[6] Hersom, born June 15, 1828; married, March 28, 1859, Charles F. Mitchell, of Freeport, Me.

789. II. Asa[6] Hersom, born December 10, 1829; married, February 12, 1852, Emily M. Parker, of Springvale, Me.; had:

790. I. Fred P.[7] Hersom, born February 12, 1853.

791. II. Frank S.[7] Hersom, born February 25, 1856; married, April 23, 1883, Carrie B. Harriman, of Providence, R. I.; had:

792. I. Frank H.[8] Hersom, born August 13, 1885.

793. III. Clement E.[7] Hersom, born October 1, 1861.

794. IV. HARRY L.[7] HERSOM, born November 4, 1868.

795. V. ASA R.[7] HERSOM, born November 10, 1870.

796. VI. CARL[7] HERSOM, born April 11, 1876.

797. III. LORENZO R.[6] HERSOM, born October 19, 1831. He is a manufacturer of leather, and merchant in wool, in Berwick; has been a director in the Somersworth National Bank of New Hampshire since 1876; was treasurer for the town of Berwick two years, and representative in the Maine State Legislature in 1877 and 1881. He married, September 21, 1854, Martha E. Tibbitts; had:

798. I. ALTON E.[7] HERSOM, born in Berwick, April 24, 1858; married, October 20, 1880, Belle Lock, of Great Falls, N. H.; had:

799. I. MARTHA[8] HERSOM, born July 27, 1881.

800. II. ASHTON[7] HERSOM, born in Berwick, December 29, 1864; died August 25, 1865.

801. III. HENRY L.[7] HERSOM, born December 16, 1868; died May 13, 1869.

802. IV. WINIFRED E.[7] HERSOM, born September 14, 1868; died December 23, 1870. Martha died September 29, 1879, and he married again Mrs. Abbie Ham Clements, of North Berwick, Me.

803. IV. ANDREW J.[6] HERSOM, born July 11, 1835; married, October 4, 1857, SUSAN P.[6] BUTLER (1012), daughter of David G.[5] (1011) and Mary S. (Pike) Butler (whom see for descendants).

804. V. ELIZABETH[6] HERSOM, born May 17, 1838; married, 1857, L. J. Perkins, late of Berwick, Me., now of Portland, Me.; had:

805. I. CARRIE ADELAIDE[7] PERKINS, born January 10, 1858; married, July 4, 1877, Henry C. Hixon, of Woodford's Deering, Me. She died August 26, 1885.

806. II. ELLA FRANCIS[7] PERKINS, born December 12, 1860; married, February 6, 1884, Philip Sheridan Mosher, of Woodford's Deering, Me.

807. III. L. J. D.[7] PERKINS, born January 1, 1862; married, December 16, 1885, Susan Maria Henry.

808. IV. LIZZIE BELLE[7] PERKINS, born December 15, 1864; married, December 16, 1885, William Edward Gilman.

809. V. FRED HERSOM[7] PERKINS, born September 18, 1866; died September 7, 1867.

810. VI. HARRY WILLIS[7] PERKINS, born June 27, 1869.

811. VII. FRANK CROCKETT[7] PERKINS, born March 25, 1873.

812. VIII. GRACE WINIFRED[7] PERKINS, born October 23, 1874.

813. II. ASA[5] HERSOM, born August 23, 1803; died July 29, 1827.

814. III. EDMUND[5] HERSOM, born May 28, 1807; died February 25, 1842.

815. IV. LYDIA[5] HERSOM, born February 3, 1813;

died July 27, 1816. Joseph[5] married again,
March, 1839, Nancy Goodwin, of Lebanon,
Me.

46.

ICHABOD[4] BUTLER, sixth child of Moses[3] and
Keziah (Nason) Butler; born in Berwick, August
27, 1775; died in Berwick, November 11, 1847.
He was a trader in Berwick; married, March 16,
1796, first, Sarah (Sally) Shorey; had :

816. I. ADAH,[5] born in Berwick, October 1, 1797;
died October 2, 1875; married Timothy Spencer, December, 1817; had :

817. I. THIRZA[6] SPENCER, born in Berwick, April
4, 1821; married Nahum Wentworth, of
Somersworth, N. H., December 4, 1845, and
died September 22, 1846.

818. II. ICHABOD B.[6] SPENCER, born in Berwick, Me.,
February 10, 1823; died February 26, 1880;
married, May 24, 1842, Lucy J. Knox, of
Lebanon; had :

819. I. HARRIET A.[7] SPENCER, born in Berwick,
August 10, 1842; married, first, December,
1860, Monroe Hyde; again, February 14, 1868,
George M. Parks, of Portsmouth, N. H.;
had :

820. I. NANCY ADELINE[8] PARKS, born January 30,
1869; died March 16, 1869.

821. II. HENRY C.[7] SPENCER, born in Berwick, April
17, 1844; died young.

822. III. THIRZA W.[7] SPENCER, born November 30, 1845; died June 11, 1859.

823. IV. HENRY C.[7] SPENCER, born in Berwick, January 15, 1849; married, June 10, 1871, Nellie Buzzell, of Vermont; had:

824. I. KATE M.[8] SPENCER, born July 5, 1872.

825. II. ARTHUR H.[8] SPENCER, born July 26, 1874.

826. III. HARRIET G.[8] SPENCER, born April 1, 1880.

827. V. EMMA E.[7] SPENCER, born in Berwick, November 1, 1850; married, July 3, 1877, George H. Carlton, of Portsmouth, N. H.; had:

828. I. CORA E.[8] CARLTON, born April 20, 1878.

829. II. GEORGE HENRY[8] CARLTON, born November 25, 1879; died July 28, 1880.

830. III. GEORGE ALBION[8] CARLTON, born February 26, 1882.

a. IV. WILLIAM WRIGHT[8] CARLTON, born December 21, 1884.

831. VI. MARY F.[7] SPENCER, born February 28, 1856; married, August 4, 1873, Jacob Mason, had:

832. I. LILLIE M.[8] MASON, born July 24, 1874.

833. II. MABEL[8] MASON, born March 6, 1876.

834. III. ALICE P.[8] MASON, born August 6, 1878.

835. IV. GEORGE C.[8] MASON, born September 29, 1880.

836. V. CORA E.[8] MASON, born October 12, 1882.

837. VI. FLORA E.[8] MASON, born September 23, 1885.

838. III. SARAH[6] SPENCER, born in Berwick, Sep-

tember 4, 1825; married, June 24, 1848, Samuel T. Parker; had:

839. I. MARY A.[7] PARKER, born October 2, 1853; married, January 9, 1872, Philip H. Stiles; had:
840. I. BLANCHE[8] STILES, born August 6, 1873.
841. II. SADIE A.[8] STILES, born July 5, 1880.
842. II. MINNIE E.[7] PARKER, born in Berwick, August 13, 1855; married, May 18, 1872, Edward E. Nelson; had:
843. I. LEON[8] NELSON, born June 11, 1873.
844. II. HERBERT[8] NELSON, born July 27, 1876.
845. III. JOSIE V.[8] NELSON, born November 15, 1885.
846. III. JOSIE B.[7] PARKER, born January 6, 1857; married, November 1, 1879, John H. Jellison, of Berwick; had:
847. I. MAUD[8] JELLISON, born in Berwick, October 2, 1880.
848. II. BERTHA[8] JELLISON, born November 10, 1881.
849. III. LAURA[8] JELLISON, born January 27, 1883.
850. IV. WILLIAM[8] JELLISON, born January 21, 1885.
851. IV. JENNIE[7] PARKER, born May 3, 1859.
852. II. MAHALA,[5] born in Berwick, September 6, 1803; died March 17, 1861; married, August 29, 1833, John Weeks, of Somersworth, N. H.; had:
853. I. MELISSA JANE[6] WEEKS, born August 10, 1834; married, first, John Thurston; had:

854. I. WILBUR H.[7] THURSTON, born July 4, 1857; married, October 7, 1880, May Boyd, of New York; had:

855. I. MELISSA[8] THURSTON, born in New York, July 6, 1881; died July 4, 1882.

856. II. ALTA BELLE[8] THURSTON, born in St. Louis, Mo., May 28, 1883.

857. III. JOHN EDWARD[8] THURSTON, born at Stoneham, Mass., August 14, 1885.

Melissa Jane[6] (853) married again, September, 1865, George Jenkins; had:

858. II. LOLA E.[7] JENKINS, born November 26, 1866.

859. II. JOSEPH DEARBORN[6] WEEKS, born August 4, 1835; died January 27, 1853.

860. III. JOHN[6] WEEKS, born March 6, 1839.

861. III. MARY,[5] born in Berwick, April 8, 1807; married, September 10, 1837, Michael E. Corson, and lives in Rochester, N. H.; had:

862. I. JOHN[6] CORSON, born May 14, 1840; married, June 13, 1871, Kate, daughter of Hon. Henry Carter, of Bradford, Mass.; had:

863. I. HENRY CARTER[7] CORSON, born June 15, 1872.

864. II. CHARLES EMERSON[7] CORSON, born August 25, 1879.

865. II. HIRAM[6] CORSON, born July 17, 1842; married, December 24, 1869, Delia D. Ham, of Cambridge, Mass.; had:

866. I. IRVING[7] CORSON, born October 4, 1871.

867. III. James[6] Corson, born February 16, 1845; married, April 3, 1877, Mary E. Curtis; had:
868. I. Freeman[7] Corson, born June 3, 1878.
869. II. Edna[7] Corson, born May 31, 1880.
870. III. Woodbury[7] Corson, born August 12, 1882; died October 6, 1885.
871. IV. Lillie May[7] Corson, born August 1, 1885.
872. IV. Nahum[6] Corson, born March 8, 1847; married, December 10, 1872, Mary J. Goodwin, of Acton, Me.

Ichabod[4] (46) married again the widow Sarah (Sally) Remick, sister of Elijah and Frederick Hays, of Berwick; she died in 1841, aged forty-eight years; had by her:

873. IV. Charles S.,[5] born in Berwick, June 24, 1834. He left Berwick at the age of seven years, on the death of his mother, and went to live in the family of his maternal uncle George W. Hays, in Somerville, Mass. At the age of seventeen he entered the store of William B. Spooner, Esq., of Boston, to whose business he has succeeded. He is a hide and leather manufacturer and merchant in Boston; married, in Boston, September 7, 1864, Elizabeth N. Cummings, born in Boston, 1841; had:
874. I. Lizzie Spooner,[6] born in Boston, January 31, 1866; died May 27, 1882.
875. II. Charles S.,[6] born in Boston, July 6, 1870.
876. III. Jennie,[6] born in Boston, March, 1872; died July, 1872.

47.

BENJAMIN[4] BUTLER, seventh child of Moses[3] and Keziah (Nason) Butler, born in Berwick, Me., August 14, 1777; married, September 11, 1799, Sarah Gowell; had:

877. I. SABINA,[5] born in Berwick, January 29, 1802; married Samuel Wade; had:

878. I. EMELINE[6] WADE, born in Berwick; married Benjamin Allen, of Berwick; had:

879. I. BENJAMIN[7] ALLEN.

880. II. EMELINE[7] ALLEN.

881. III. EMMA[7] ALLEN.

882. II. SERENA,[5] born with Sabina, January 29, 1802; died young.

883. III. DOROTHY,[5] born in Berwick, 1803; died April 2, 1885; married, March 25, 1823, William Huntress, of Dover, N. H. He was born February 10, 1801; died October 16, 1855. Their children are:

884. I. SERENA B.[6] HUNTRESS, born February 2, 1824; married Lawrence Gould; had:

885. I. ISABELLA[7] GOULD.

886. II. FLORA[7] GOULD.

887. III. SARAH[7] GOULD.

888. IV. LEANDER[7] GOULD.

889. V. AMANDA[7] GOULD.

890. II. LEANDER S.[6] HUNTRESS, born in Dover, N. H., October 17, 1825. He was for many years chief engineer in the service of a New York

and Panama line of steamers; is now a dentist
in Dover, N. H.; married, October 30, 1873,
Hannah E. Dam; had:

891. I. LUCINDA G.[7] HUNTRESS, born in Dover, N.
H., August 13, 1874.

892. II. LEON DANIEL [7] HUNTRESS, born in Dover,
May 18, 1885; died January 4, 1886.

893. III. SARAH E.[6] HUNTRESS, born in Dover, N
H., December 16, 1827; died September 21,
1831.

894. IV. ANGELIA[6] HUNTRESS, born in Dover, May
16, 1828; married Isaac Farrar; had:

895. I. GELIETTA[7] FARRAR, married, first, Joseph
Richardson; had one son. She married again
in 1877, Edmond Perkins.

896. V. MARY FRANCES[6] HUNTRESS, born in Dover,
N. H., July 16, 1829; married, in Lawrence,
Mass., September 18, 1850, Charles Emerson.
They live in Washington, D. C.; had:

897. I. MARY HORNER[7] EMERSON, born in Dover,
July 5, 1854; married, July 5, 1876, James F.
Hood, of Ohio; had:

898. I. CHARLES EMERSON[8] HOOD, born July 30,
1878.

899. II. ROLLIN MORGAN[8] HOOD, born August 31,
1882.

900. III. FRANCES LOUISE[8] HOOD, born September
16, 1884; died July 27, 1885. These were
all born in Washington.

901. II. SARAH DOROTHY[7] EMERSON, born in Wash-

ington, January 6, 1860; died January 27, 1865.

902. VI. GEORGE H.[6] HUNTRESS, born in Dover, N. H., March 25, 1831; died July 27, 1845.

903. VII. SARAH E.[6] HUNTRESS, born in Dover, N. H., April 3, 1833; married John Shepley, of Providence, R. I., born in 1823, and died December 20, 1874; had:

904. I. GEORGE L.[7] SHEPLEY, born in Dover, N. H., October 11, 1854; married, September 15, 1880, Carrie Peck.

905. II. ALICE[7] SHEPLEY, born in Providence, R. I., June 5, 1857; married, November 10, 1880, Thomas A. Richardson.

906. III. HATTIE M.[7] SHEPLEY, born in Providence, R. I., October 3, 1859; died February 4, 1864.

907. IV. MARY L.[7] SHEPLEY, born in Providence, R. I., October 1, 1862; died young.

908. VIII. WILLIAM B.[6] HUNTRESS, born in Dover, N. H., September 1, 1834; married, and had:

909. I. NELLIE[7] HUNTRESS, born in New York.

910. II. WILLIAM[7] HUNTRESS, born in New York.

911. IX. DOROTHY A.[6] HUNTRESS, born in Dover, N. H., December 9, 1835; died September 13, 1836.

912. X. CHARLES A.[6] HUNTRESS, born in Dover, N. H., May 8, 1838; died in Washington, April 29, 1869; married, November 26, 1857, Lizzie Williams; had:

913. I. ELIZABETH W.[7] HUNTRESS, born in Washington, September 10, 1858; married, April 9, 1876, John F. Fuller; had :

914. I. CARRIE MAY[8] FULLER, born in Washington, November 27, 1876.

915. II. CHARLES F.[8] FULLER, born in Washington, September 17, 1878.

916. III. GRACE L.[8] FULLER, born in Washington, March 4, 1883.

917. II. HARRIET LOUISE[7] HUNTRESS, born in Washington, March 22, 1861.

918. III. CHARLES A.[7] HUNTRESS, born in Washington, July 4, 1869; died February 3, 1880.

919. XI. ELLEN A.[6] HUNTRESS, born in Dover, N. H., May 2, 1841; died August 2, 1848.

920. XII. AMANDA J.[6] HUNTRESS, born with Ellen A.,[6] May 2, 1841; married, November 7, 1861, first, Lorenzo Connor. He was killed in battle at Fort Wagner, July 18, 1863; had one child, died in infancy. She married again, September 26, 1866, Ira N. Colby; had :

921. I. MABEL H.[7] COLBY, born in Warner, N. H., October 5, 1869.

922. II. HENRY L.[7] COLBY, born in Fisherville, N. H., April 20, 1873.

923. III. GEORGE B.[7] COLBY, born in Boscawen, N. H., August 20, 1878.

924. IV. FRED. E.[7] COLBY, born in Boscawen, N. H., January 24, 1884.

925. IV. MARY,[5] born in Berwick, 1805; married

November 7, 1822, John Hooper, of South
Berwick; had:

926. I. SHELDON[6] HOOPER, born in South Berwick,
August, 1822.

927. II. ADAH B.[6] HOOPER, born in South Berwick,
March 3, 1825; died February 28, 1884; married, June 4, 1843, Charles F. Abbott. He
was born October 9, 1817; had:

928. I. ELLEN A.[7] ABBOTT, born April 21, 1844;
married, August 8, 1866, Charles A. Littlefield, of Somerville, Mass., where they reside;
no issue.

929. II. SAMUEL B.[7] ABBOTT, born April 3, 1845;
married, March 25, 1875, Almeda V. Hayes,
of West Lebanon, Me.; had:

930. I. FLORENCE A.[8] ABBOTT, born January 24,
1877; died July 27, 1879.

931. II. FRED HAYES[8] ABBOTT, born with Florence
A.,[8] January 24, 1877.

932. III. MABEL L.[8] ABBOTT, born September 1,
1878.

933. IV. RAYMOND B.[8] ABBOTT, born February 1,
1885.

934. III. CHARLES O.[7] ABBOTT, born September 7,
1846.

935. IV. MARY A.[7] ABBOTT, born June 5, 1851;
died April 29, 1858.

936. V. SHELDON H.[7] ABBOTT, born April 19, 1859.

937. III. SUSAN[6] HOOPER, born in South Berwick;
died young.

938. IV. M. Augusta[6] Hooper, married ———— Pilsbury; had:

939. I. Etta[7] Pilsbury.

940. V. Anna[6] Hooper, born in South Berwick.

941. VI. Harriet[6] Hooper, born in South Berwick; married John Dolloff; had:

942. I. Admina[7] Dolloff (and one who died young).

943. VII. Mary Frances[6] Hooper; married William Keay; had:

944. I. Lizzie[7] Keay.

945. VIII. John Albert[6] Hooper, born in South Berwick; married Fanny Goodwin.

946. IX. Sarah E.[6] Hooper; married ———— Standen; had:

947. I. Ida[7] Standen.

948. II. Emma[7] Standen.

949. III. Julia[7] Standen.

950. IV. Frank[7] Standen.

951. V. Thomas,[5] born in Berwick, 1807; lived in New York; was a contractor of railroad bridges, etc.; married April 17, 1836, Harriet Benedict; she was born May 30, 1813; had:

952. I. Joseph Benedict,[6] born in Brooklyn, N. Y.; was a volunteer in the New York Seventy-first Regiment, and was killed in battle of Bull Run. And two others.

953. VI. Frances,[5] born in Berwick, 1809; married Samuel Hall; had:

954. I. George[6] Hall, died in Baltimore, Md.

7

955. II. Armenia [6] Hall, born in Berwick; married July 2, 1848, William F. Wentworth, son of Samuel and Rachel (Furbush) Wentworth, of Lebanon; he was born August 21, 1823; had (besides those who died in infancy):

956. I. Fannie L.[7] Wentworth, born February 8, 1849.

957. II. Sarah A.[7] Wentworth, born May 18, 1851; married October, 1870, Marcena Lane.

958. III. William H.[7] Wentworth, born May 21, 1857.

959. IV. Samuel H.[7] Wentworth, born February 24, 1859.

960. V. Julia A.[7] Wentworth, born November 23, 1861.

961. VI. George E.[7] Wentworth, born March 18, 1866.

962. III. Samuel [6] Hall.

963. VII. Benjamin,[5] born in Berwick, went to South Carolina and there died by accident.

964. VIII. John,[5] born in 1812; married first Hannah Randall of North Berwick; again Abby Dearborn; had by first wife:

965. I. Harriet,[6] born in Berwick, 1835.

966. II. Martha,[6] born in Berwick, 1837; died single.

967. III. John,[6] born June 7, 1839; died single.

968. IV. Benjamin,[6] born in Berwick, May 28, 1841; married Georgia Brooks, of Salmon Falls, N. H.; had one child, Herbert,[7] died young.

969. V. J. F.,[6] born in Berwick, February 15, 1844; graduated at Bates College, Lewiston, Me., in the class of 1863 ; during his course in college he taught the winter school of Wells, Me., in 1860 and 1861 ; and in the Winter of 1863 he taught the school in Somersworth, N. H.; and in Berwick, Me., in 1864. Mr. Butler is at present a resident of Brooklyn, N. Y., and a manufacturer in New York City; he married Celia E. Rice; born in Portland, Me., January 1, 1843 ; had:

970. I. ALICE G.,[7] born in Portland, Me., May, 1868.

971. II. J. F.,[7] born in Brooklyn, N. Y., December, 1879.

972. IX. LYDIA,[5] born in Berwick, Me., May 13, 1816; married, January 17, 1838, Allen Hall, born June 10, 1814 ; had:

973. I. BENJAMIN B.[6] HALL, born in Berwick, Me., May 19, 1839. Lives in Charlestown, Mass. Married, December 28, 1880, Parthenia Burns, of Portsmouth, N. H.; had :

a. I. EDNA F.[7] HALL, born in Boston, March 11, 1884.

974. II. JULIA A.[6] HALL, born in Lebanon, Me., April 30, 1842 ; married, July 15, 1869, Charles M. Stewart, of East Corinth, Me.; had:

a. I. IDA M.[7] STEWART, born in East Corinth, Me., November 8, 1875.

a. II. Isa F.[7] Stewart, born with Ida M.,[7] November 8, 1875.

975. III. Hazen A.[6] Hall, born in Lebanon, Me., July 10, 1843; married, October 25, 1876, Opalina Powell, of Philadelphia; had:

a. I. Ida G.[7] Hall, born in Philadelphia, September 25, 1878.

a. II. Opalina P.[7] Hall, born in Philadelphia, July 14, 1881.

976. IV. Sarah J.[6] Hall, born in Lebanon, November 4, 1848; died, April 8, 1850.

977. V. George O.[6] Hall, born in Lebanon, May 20, 1846; is a dentist in Boston; married, October 15, 1876, Almira F. Frisbee.

978. VI. Harriet E.[6] Hall, born in Lebanon, May 14, 1847; died July 22, 1872.

979. VII. Charles A.[6] Hall, born in Lebanon, December 2, 1849; married in Boston, October 15, 1873, Mary O. Todd; had:

a. I. Gertrude F.[7] Hall, born in Boston, July 19, 1874.

A. VIII. Sarah J.[6] Hall again, born August 31, 1851; died September 24, 1851.

A. IX. Franklin E.[6] Hall, born April 3, 1853; died September 5, 1853.

A. X. Imogene F.[6] Hall, born in Lebanon, May 11, 1855; married, June 30, 1874, Clarence C. Wharff, of Damariscotta, Me.; had:

a. Alice V.[7] Wharff, born in Boston, May 26, 1882.

A. XI. WAYLAND F.[6] HALL, born in Lebanon, July 2, 1856; married, August 8, 1878, Lizzie A. Tibbitts, of Lynn, Mass.; had:

a. I. EDITH M.[7] HALL, born in Boston, November 3, 1880.

A. XII. IDA E.[6] HALL, born in Lebanon, Me., March 13, 1858; married, September 15, 1881, Frederick H. Talcott; he is a dentist in Boston.

980. X. SARAH,[5] born in. Berwick, May 5, 1818; married, November 22, 1842, George Guptill, of Berwick; had:

981. I. JAMES[6] GUPTILL, born in Berwick, August 11, 1843; died young.

982. II. MARY F.[6] GUPTILL, born in Berwick, July 30, 1845; died young.

983. III. MELISSA[6] GUPTILL, born December 15, 1847; died young.

984. IV. AMANDA J.[6] GUPTILL, born June 1, 1849; married Henry Clements, of Berwick; had:

985. I. FRANK[7] CLEMENTS, born in Berwick, June, 1867.

986. V. HOLLIS[6] GUPTILL, born in Berwick, October 30, 1851; married, January 26, 1874, Lizzie Woolley; had:

987. I. GRACE[7] GUPTILL.

988. VI. MARY A.[6] GUPTILL, born in Berwick, August 6, 1852; married, November 24, 1874, Josiah Walker.

989. VII. LYDIA F.[6] GUPTILL, born in Berwick,

January 12, 1854; married, November, 1875, Henry Hill.

990. VIII. LEANDER[6] GUPTILL, born December 1, 1856; died young.

991. IX. GEORGE L.[6] GUPTILL, born in Berwick, April 24, 1859.

992. X. NELLIE E.[6] GUPTILL, born in Berwick, July 8, 1862.

48.

NATHAN[4] BUTLER, eighth child of Moses[3] and Keziah (Nason) Butler, born in Berwick, September 20, 1779. He lived on a farm in Berwick in early life, where all of his children were born, and where his first wife died. Later he removed to Whitestown, N. Y., where he died. He married, first, in 1801, Adah Chick; she was born in 1779 and died in 1836. He married again, in 1838, Sally W. Paul; had (all by first wife):

993. I. ALVAN,[5] born July 9, 1803; died September 18, 1828.

994. II. NATHAN,[5] born February 19, 1807; died August 30, 1828.

995. III. Rev. OLIVER,[5] born February 25, 1809. He lived with his parents until sixteen years of age, when he entered a store in Great Falls, N. H., as clerk. He continued in this capacity until twenty-one years old, when he opened a store of general merchandise on his own ac-

count. He maintained this business for nine years, during which time he was appointed trial justice, and had a large number of cases brought before him. In 1838 he gave up his mercantile pursuits, to teach the village school on the Berwick side of the river. In 1840 he removed to Parsonsfield, Me., and entered the theological school there to prepare for the ministry. He was ordained a minister of the Gospel in the Freewill Baptist Church at Great Falls in 1843, and entered upon the work of the ministry at Effingham Falls, then a new place without a church or house to worship in. Mr. Butler continued in this, his parish, eight years, during which time his congregation erected a new house of worship. Since then he has accepted the following pastorates: Wolfsborough, N. H., two years; Middleton, N. H., one year; Andover, N. H., three years; Phillipsburg, Me., one year; Meredith Centre, N. H., twelve years; Buxton, Me., three years; Lyman, Me., one year. In 1872 Mr. Butler bought a part interest in a publishing house at Biddeford, Me., in which was published the *Union and Journal*, Republican paper of York County, Me. He continued in this business five years, and during this time preached on the Sabbath in various churches. In 1879 he opened a new printing establishment, and started a new *independent* paper called the

Biddeford Weekly Advance, which he afterward sold. He is now retired and living in Chelsea, Mass. He married, about 1830, Merriam S., daughter of the Rev. Elijah Watson, of Sutton, N. H.; had (besides three who died young):

996. I. MARILLA J.,[6] born in Berwick, June 2, 1833; is a graduate of the New Hampton Seminary, 1857, and is now living in Salem, Mass.

997. II. HON. JOHN EDWARD,[6] born in Berwick, Me., July 6, 1836. He graduated at Bowdoin College in the class of '61. Became editor of the *Union and Journal*, a leading newspaper in Western Maine, and settled in Biddeford. He was admitted to the bar in 1865. Held various positions of influence and trust in the political party to which he belonged; was elected to the Maine Senate from York County in 1873, and was President of that body in 1874 and 1875. He was for five years the chief attorney in Maine for the Eastern Railroad, and the president's confidential legal adviser. After sixteen years of editorial labor he removed to Boston, to devote himself to his old practice of law, which he had laid aside to take up the pen of journalism, and where he has a very large practice. He married Anna M., daughter of Thomas J. and Eliza Robinson, of Laconia, N. H.; had:

998. I. ESTELLE M.,[7] born May 14, 1862; was a

graduate of the Chelsea High School, and died October 11, 1882.

999. II. RALPH EDWARD,[7] born July 11, 1871.

1000. IV. REV. JOHN J.,[5] A.M., D.D., born in Berwick, Me., April 9, 1814. He entered the South Berwick Academy at the age of seventeen years, and prepared for college here and at the Parsonsfield Seminary; in 1834 he entered Bowdoin College in the Sophomore Class, and graduated in 1837. He was assistant teacher in the Parsonsfield Seminary one year following his graduation, and was principal of the Farmington Academy in 1838 and 1839; was principal of the Clinton Seminary, New York, in 1841 and 1842. Dr. Butler had cherished from early youth the hope of entering the ministry of the Gospel, and in 1844 he graduated from the Andover Theological Seminary in the class with President Bartlett, of Dartmouth College, H. M. Dexter, D.D., of Boston, and Dr. R. S. Storrs, of Brooklyn, N. Y. Immediately after graduation he was elected Professor of Biblical Theology in the Theological School at Whitestown, N. Y. He filled this chair for ten years, till 1854, when he accepted the chair of Systematic Theology at the New Hampton Seminary, N. H., in which he continued until 1870, when he was chosen Professor of Theology in Bates College, Me. In

1873 he was elected Professor of Sacred
Literature in Hillsdale College, Mich., which
position he held until 1883. In 1866, Dr.
Butler's health becoming somewhat impaired,
owing to continued labors, seemed to call for
a rest from so close application, and he was
granted a recess from his labors for a year.
During this vacation he made a tour of
Europe, occupying eight months. In 1849
he received the degree of A.M. from Hamilton College, and in 1860 Bowdoin College
conferred on him the degree of D.D. Besides
much which he has written for the press, he
has been an editorial contributor to the
Morning Star for over fifty years. In 1860
he published *Natural and Revealed Theology*,
a work of 450 pages, which has been adopted
as a standard and text-book by the Free
Baptist denomination; two volumes of com-
mentaries on the New Testament of 490 pages,
published in 1870-71, besides several smaller
works, and is now engaged on another work
of similar import as the first three volumes.
He married, November 14, 1844, Elizabeth,
daughter of the Rev. Dr. Robert Everett, a
Welsh divine and author, late of Remsen,
N. Y. She was born in 1818, in Wales,
Great Britain, and died in Hillsdale, Mich.,
April 11, 1877; had:

1001. I. REV. JOHN H.,[6] A.M., born in Whitestown,

N. Y.. October 1, 1849, prepared for college at the New Hampton Institute, and graduated at Dartmouth College in the class of '73. He was Professor of Latin in Hillsdale College from 1876 to 1880. He also taught one year in Mexico, N. Y. He entered the Union Theological Seminary, New York, in 1882, and graduated in the class of '85. Received a call to the Congregational Church at Moriah, N. Y., and was ordained there, September 2, 1885. He married, March 3, 1877, Amanda Bentley, of Mantua, O.

1002. II. LIZZIE L.,[6] born at Whitestown, N. Y., September 28, 1852. She graduated at the Lewiston High School in 1872 ; married, August 11, 1873, Frank Sands, of Lewiston, Me.; had :

1003. I. ELLA CLARA[7] SANDS, born in Hillsdale, October 24, 1874.

1004. II. EVERETT[7] SANDS, born in 1878.

1005. III. HATTIE E.,[6] born in New Hampton, N. H., May 2, 1855, graduated at Hillsdale College, class of '76.

1006. V. LOUISA,[5] born in Berwick, Me., December 19, 1819 ; married, April 21, 1846, William H.[6] Thompson (385), son of Olive[5] (384) (Butler) Thompson, born February 9, 1824 ; had :

1007. I. HENRY MARTIN[6] THOMPSON, born in Portsmouth, N. H., February 19, 1847 ; married,

September 12, 1872, Nellie, youngest daughter of the late Governor Straw, of New Hampshire. He is the owner and manager of the Lowell Felting Mills; had:

1008. I. ALBERT WILLIAM[7] THOMPSON.
1009. II. HERMAN ELLIS[7] THOMPSON.
1010. II. EMMA OLIVE[6] THOMPSON, born in Portsmouth, N. H.; died in Biddeford, Me., August 13, 1851.
1011. III. ALICE MARILLA[6] THOMPSON, born in Biddeford, Me., September 3, 1853; died September 23, 1858.

50.

JAMES[4] BUTLER, tenth child of Moses[3] and Keziah (Nason) Butler, born in Berwick, January 17, 1783; died January 21, 1856; married, 1804, Hannah Grant; had:

1012. I. LOIS,[5] born in Berwick, November 18, 1805; died without issue, June 9, 1829; married Hawley Applebee, January 15, 1829.
1013. II. EDMOND,[5] born August 5, 1807; died June 18, 1850; married, July 3, 1835, Betsey Frost; had:
1014. I. STEPHEN,[6] born in Berwick, November 6, 1836; married Sarah A. Howard; had:
1015. I. ELLA,[7] born in Berwick, February 28, 1856.
1016. II. CHARLES C.,[7] born in Berwick, July 28, 1858.

1017. III. GEORGE H.,[7] born in Berwick, March 6, 1861 ; died young.

1018. IV. FANNIE,[7] born in Berwick, September 6, 1862.

   a. II. LYDIA,[6] died young.

   b. III. LOIS,[6] is single.

   c. IV. SARAH HANNAH,[6] married Charles Lovejoy.

1019. III. EZRA,[5] born in Berwick, March 5, 1809 ; married, May 12, 1831, Mary Grant, of Acton, Me.; had :

1020. I. JONATHAN G.,[6] born in Berwick, February 12, 1832.

1021. II. JOHN FRANCIS,[6] born in Berwick, September 12, 1834 ; married, October 5, 1856, Nancy T. Neal; had :

1022. I. CHARLES J.,[7] born October 11, 1857 ; died March 19, 1885.

   John Francis [6] married again, October 23, 1880, Mrs. Mary Ellen Whitehouse, of North Berwick, Me.

1023. IV. DAVID G.,[5] born in Berwick, January 5, 1813 ; lived in Berwick until 1857 ; was a timber and lumber manufacturer and merchant. He is now retired and lives in Great Falls, N. H. ; married, June 21, 1835, Mary S., daughter of Elias and Susan (Bean) Pike, of Waterborough, Me.; had :

1024. I. SUSAN PIKE,[6] born in Berwick, May 24, 1836 ; married, October 4, 1857, Andrew J.[6] Hersom (803), of Lebanon ; had :

1025. I. ADELAIDE L.[7] HERSOM, born in Berwick,
July 2, 1862; married, January 24, 1884,
Walter S. Allerton, Esq., a lawyer in New
York. Lives in Mount Vernon, N. Y.; had:

1026. I. ADELAIDE H.[8] ALLERTON, born in Brooklyn,
N. Y., November 19, 1884.

1027. II. GEORGE A.[7] HERSOM, born in Berwick,
July 16, 1865; died young.

1028. II. GEORGE H.,[6] born in Berwick, May 31,
1841, was educated in the Great Falls High
School. He taught the winter term of school
in Ossipee, N. H., in 1861. The following
spring he entered the office of the late Dr.
Buzzell, of Dover, N. H., a student in medicine. The following year, Dr. Buzzell having
accepted an appointment of Assistant Surgeon
in one of the New Hampshire regiments then
at the seat of war, he continued his studies
in the office and under the instruction of the
late Dr. Alfonso Bickford, then Mayor of
Dover. While with Dr. Bickford he taught
the winter term of one of the district schools
in Dover, and attended a course of lectures
at the Bowdoin Medical School, and a second
course at the medical department of the University of Pennsylvania in Philadelphia in
1863-64. Before the close of this term, January 9, 1864, he received an appointment of
Acting Assistant Surgeon in the United States
Navy, and was ordered immediately to the

United States Steamer Kineo, then at Baltimore, fitting out for the West Gulf Blockading Squadron under Admiral Farragut, in charge of her medical and surgical department. This of course deprived him of the opportunity of taking the degree of M.D. at the spring commencement, as he had intended. He served on the Kineo and Mahaska in this capacity for two years and a half, when he was promoted to the grade of Acting Passed Assistant Surgeon, in which capacity he continued until November 12, 1868, when he received an " Honorable Discharge " from the Navy Department. During this time he availed himself of opportunities of attending lectures at the medical schools of Baltimore, New Orleans, and Boston. On leaving the Navy he entered Bellevue Hospital Medical College and graduated in the class of '69 and commenced the practice of medicine in New York City at once. He is the author of some miscellaneous papers on medical subjects and of this work. He married, June 13, 1872, Henrietta L. Grand, daughter of the late Hon. Samuel Lawrence, of New York; had:

1029. I. WILLIAM LAWRENCE.[7]
1030. II. LAWRENCE D.[7] Both died in infancy.
1031. III. HORACE P.,[6] born in Berwick, March 24, 1843; is a lawyer. He graduated at the

Great Falls High School in the class of '61; taught district schools both in Maine and New Hampshire; read law with the late Daniel M. Christie, Esq., of Dover, N. H.; graduated at the Law School in Albany, N. Y.; was admitted to the bar and practised in North Carolina and Tennessee; married Rose, daughter of Jethro Furber, of Wolfsborough, N. H.; no issue.

1032. IV. DAVID FRANKLIN,[6] born in Berwick, December 18, 1848. He was educated at the Great Falls High School and at Poughkeepsie, N. Y.; married, March 28, 1874, Olive Grant, of Berwick; she was born September 25, 1848; had:

1033. I. MARY EDNA,[7] born in Great Falls, N. H., August 31, 1875.

1034. II. DAVID IRWIN,[7] born October 20, 1876; died December 3, 1877.

1035. III. GRACE BERTHA,[7] born June 22, 1878.

1036. IV. GEORGE H.,[7] born December 29, 1881.

1037. V. MINNIE BELLE,[7] born December 8, 1885.

1038. V. EUNICE,[5] born in Berwick, March 28, 1815; died December 26, 1850; married Horatio N. Mathews; certificate granted March 29, 1834; had:

1039. I. JAMES [6] MATHEWS, born in Dover, N. H.; December 17, 1835; married, July 12, 1857, Ann Day; had:

1040. I. CRISSIE A.[7] MATHEWS, born June 17, 1860

1041. II. CHARLES H.[7] MATHEWS, born April 9, 1862; died August 10, 1875.

1042. II. CHARLES W.[6] MATHEWS, born in Berwick, December 31, 1841; married November 14, 1864, Annie Clarkson, of Elliott, Me.

1043. III. MARY ANN[6] MATHEWS, born in Berwick, Me., May 18, 1843; married, May, 1860, Charles Plummer, of Somersworth, N. H.; had (besides two who died young):

1044. I. CHARLES[7] PLUMMER, born April 9, 1863.

1045. VI. CAPT. JAMES,[5] born in Berwick, March 15, 1817; died August 2, 1880; married, July 9, 1840, Betsy, daughter of Philip Hall, of Berwick, Me.; had:

1046. I. MARY FRANCES,[6] born in Berwick, September 16, 1842; married, May, 1871, George B. White, of Boston, Mass.

1047. II. ORIN H.,[6] born May 29, 1844; married, May 2, 1868, Ora A. Chellis, of Great Falls, N. H.; had:

1048. I. ARTHUR CHELLIS,[7] born in Berwick, June 29, 1869.

1049. II. LILLIAN G.,[7] born in Berwick, January 23, 1871.

1050. III. HERVEY SMITH,[7] born February 9, 1872; died July 26, 1872.

1051. IV. EFFIE MAY,[7] born September 15, 1873.

1052. V. CLARENCE ORIN,[7] born October 16, 1875.

1053. VI. JESSIE FLORENCE,[7] born August 29, 1880.

1054. VII. WINIFRED ETHEL,[7] born July 11, 1884.

8

1055. III. PHILIP H.,[6] born in Berwick, February
2, 1847; married, November 12, 1879, Emma
Merrill. He is a merchant in Boston, Mass.;
They had :

1056. I. MERRILL PHILIP,[7] born October 6, 1880.

1057. II. ELIZABETH,[7] born April 8, 1883.

1058. IV. JOSIE AUGUSTA,[6] born in Berwick, January 17, 1849 ; married, June 6, 1872, Edwin
Fernald, some time editor and proprietor
of the *Great Falls Journal*, now engaged
in editorial work in Minneapolis, Minn. ; had :

1059. I. BLANCHE[7] FERNALD, born in Great Falls,
N. H., September 25, 1874.

1060. II. BESSIE LEONA[7] FERNALD, born in Great
Falls, N. H., January 30, 1877.

1061. III. MADGE[7] FERNALD, born in St. Louis,
Mo., October 16, 1884.

1062. V. JAMES HENRY,[6] born in Berwick, March
29, 1851 ; married, June 17, 1884, Nellie
Goodwin, of Acton, Me.

1063. VI. ALVIN,[6] born June 29, 1853 ; married
Josephine Headly, of Minneapolis, Minn. ;
had :

1064. I. LOTTIE.[7]

1065. VII. FRED,[6] born in Berwick, May 6, 1856.

1066. VIII. EMMA,[6] born in Berwick, July 29, 1858.

1067. IX. HERBERT E.,[6] born in Berwick, September 19, 1861.

1068. VII. MARY,[5] born in Berwick, February 22,
1819 ; died September 24, 1840.

1069. VIII. John G.,[5] born in Berwick, March 31, 1821; died August 10, 1884; married, October 20, 1844, Elvira Ricker (548), daughter of Thomas and Mary Ricker, of Lebanon. She died January 3, 1850; had:

1070. I. Thomas R.,[6] born in Berwick, September 20, 1846; married, April 30, 1867, Sarah Tufts Moulton, of Andover, Mass.; had:

1071. I. Frank W.,[7] born May 4, 1870.

1072. II. Elmer,[7] born October 28, 1872.

1073. III. Philip,[7] born September 4, 1874.

1074. IV. Warren Moulton,[7] born June 2, 1876.

1075. V. Mary Louisa,[7] born March 3, 1879.

1076. IX. Hannah,[5] born in Berwick, April 23, 1823; died April 7, 1854; married George W.[6] Andrews (311), and had two children; both died in infancy.

1077. X. Moses William,[5] born in Berwick, April 21, 1825; married, December 12, 1848, Mary E.[6] (325), daughter of Daniel and (Eliza[5] (310) Goodwin) Andrews; had:

1078. I. Eliza Ann,[6] born in Berwick, December 26, 1849; married, March 24, 1869, Edward S. Thompson; had:

1079. I. Fannie[7] Thompson, born in Berwick, September 29, 1870.

1080. II. Edna[7] Thompson, born in Berwick, November 30, 1871.

1081. III. Oscar[7] Thompson, born in Berwick, March, 1873.

1082. IV. Frank[7] Thompson, born in Berwick, November, 1874.

1083. V. Charles[7] Thompson, born in Berwick, July 10, 1876.

1084. VI. Forrest[7] Thompson, born in Berwick, November, 1878.

1085. II. Mary E.,[6] born in Berwick, February 15, 1851.

1086. III. Frances E.,[6] born September 28, 1852.

1087. IV. Florence E.,[6] born with Frances, September 28, 1852.

1088. V. James W.,[6] born in Berwick, March 28, 1856.

1089. VI. Thomas J.,[6] born in Berwick, January 16, 1859.

1090. VII. Daniel G.,[6] born in Berwick, July 26, 1861.

51.

LOIS[4] BUTLER, eleventh child of Moses[3] and Keziah (Nason) Butler, born in Berwick, April 2, 1786; married, first, Charles Brown; had:

1091. I. Samuel[5] Brown, married Emeline Burbank; had:

1092. I. Charles Henry[6] Brown.

1093. II. Mary Frances[6] Brown, married ———— Perham; had:

1094. I. Emeline Frances[7] Perham.

1095. II. Alice Gertrude[7] Perham.

1096. III. Arthur Ellsworth[7] Perham.

1097. IV. Laura Clinton [7] Perham.

1098. V. Albert Clifton [7] Perham.

1099. III. George W. [6] Brown.

1100. II. Elisha [5] Brown, married, first, Elmira Whiting; second, Mrs. Livermore; had by first wife:

1101. I. Elisha James [6] Brown, born in Charlestown, Mass.; married Helen Streeter.

1102. II. Charles E. [6] Brown, born in Charlestown, Mass.; married Ellen M. Potter.

1103. III. Susan [5] Brown, married Clark Jones; had:

1104. I. Martha Ann [6] Jones.

1105. II. Charles C. [6] Jones, married Eliza A. Hartford; had:

1106. I. Helen B. [7] Jones.

1107. II. Francis H. [7] Jones.

1108. III. Charles [7] Jones.

1109. IV. Carrie [7] Jones.

1110. V. Edwin [7] Jones.

1111. VI. Minnie [7] Jones.

1112. III. Susan J. [6] Jones, married Roderick T. Abbott; had:

1113. I. John Wesley [7] Abbott.

1114. II. Lloyd Freeman [7] Abbott.

1115. III. Charles P. [7] Abbott.

1116. IV. Martha Ann [7] Abbott.

1117. V. Mary J. [7] Abbott.

1118. VI. Sally Leonora [7] Abbott.

1119. IV. Mary F. [6] Jones, married John A.

Murdock; had two children; both died young.

1120. V. WILLIAM W.⁶ JONES; married Laura Savage; had:

1121. I. EDWIN RODNEY⁷ JONES.

1122. IV. NATHAN⁵ BROWN, born November 11, 1811; married first, March 12, 1835, Comfort Stevens; died January 21, 1863; second, M. D. Burleigh, November 3, 1863; had:

1123. I. MARY JANE⁶ BROWN, born August 18, 1837; married ——— Moulton; had one child, ETTA⁷ MOULTON.

1124. II. ANN ELIZABETH⁶ BROWN, born April 25, 1840; married Orin B. Marston, of Arlington, Mass.; had:

1125. I. NELLIE⁷ MARSTON, born in Arlington, Mass.

1126. III. GEORGE E.⁶ BROWN, born July 8, 1853; married Ida Buzzell, of Newfield, Me., and resides in Lowell, Mass.; had:

1127. I. GEORGE HERBERT⁷ BROWN.

1128. II. WILLIS⁷ BROWN.

1129. III. HARRY⁷ BROWN.

1130. V. EDWIN⁵ BROWN, born 1815; died, February 20, 1842; married Betsy Stevens; had:

1131. I. CHARLES EDWIN⁶ BROWN.

1132. II. ABBIE ANN⁶ BROWN.

1133. VI. JAMES⁵ BROWN, died at the age of four years.

1134. VII. James T.[5] Brown, again, died October 7, 1864; married Rebecca Haseltine; had:

1135. I. Sarah Jane[6] Brown, born January 21, 1844; married William Nutz, of Philadelphia, Pa.; had:

1136. I. Emma L.[7] Nutz, born November 28, 1864; died February 27, 1881.

1137. II. Elizabeth[6] Brown.

1138. III. Alonzo[6] Brown.

1139. VIII. John[5] Brown, married Jane Cheesman; had:

1140. I. Frank[6] Brown.

By her second husband, Joseph Goodrich, Lois[4]; had:

1141. IX. Charles B.[5] Goodrich; is a merchant in Charlestown, Mass.; married, first, Jane Abbott; second, Abbie Lord; had by first wife:

1142. I. Charles Warren[6] Goodrich; died young.

1143. II. George B.[6] Goodrich; died young.

1144. III. Frank W.[6] Goodrich.

1145. X. Temperance[5] Goodrich, born January 23, 1826; married, July 13, 1852, Monroe Emery, of Waterborough, Me.; had:

1146. I. Samuel B.[6] Emery, born February 1, 1854; died June 14, 1866.

1147. II. George Henry[6] Emery, born July 14, 1856; married, August 17, 1877, Ellen M. Patten; had:

1148. I. Maude M.[7] Emery, born January 23, 1880.

1149. III. Frank A.[6] Emery, born July 13, 1858.

1150. XI. MARTHA ANN[5] GOODRICH, born June 14,
1827; married, January 29, 1850, Jeremiah
Shaw; had:

1151. I. JOSHUA HOLBROOK[6] SHAW, born in North
Weymouth, December 2, 1850.

1152. II. CHARLES WARREN GOODRICH[6] SHAW, born
in North Weymouth, April 14, 1853; married,
February, 1877, Mary Johnson.

1153. III. MARY ELIZABETH[6] SHAW, born in North
Weymouth, May 31, 1855; married, November 23, 1878, Emory Lester Cushing.

1154. IV. ANNA[6] SHAW, born in Weymouth, July
7, 1857.

1155. V. JACOB[6] SHAW, born October 16, 1860.

1156. VI. GEORGIE MARIA[6] SHAW, born June 30,
1863.

1157. VII. JAMES[6] SHAW, born June 25, 1868.

1158. VIII. MARTHA JANE[6] SHAW, born February
9, 1873.

1159. XII. MARY JANE[5] GOODRICH, born June 14,
1830; died August 1, 1871; married December 19, 1850, A. Clark; had:

1160. I. DR. RUFUS O.[6] CLARK, born May 22, 1852;
graduated at the Boston Dental College with
the degree of DD.S., in 1882, and is engaged
in the practice of his profession in Marlboro',
Mass.; married, December 19, 1872, Abbie
H. Morse; had:

1161. I. ESTELL MAY[7] CLARK, born February 4,
1874; died young.

1162. II. ETHEL G.[7] CLARK, born August 14, 1876;
died an infant.

1163. III. LILLA M.[7] CLARK, born February 1, 1879.

1164. II. ALBERT L.[6] CLARK, born October, 1854;
died young.

1165. III. FRANK A.[6] CLARK, born October, 1856;
married ———— Holden, of Worcester, Mass.;
had, besides one who died young:

1166. I. FRANK[7] CLARK, born in Worcester, September, 1881.

1167. II. CHARLES[7] CLARK, born in Worcester,
1885.

1168. IV. JENNIE[6] CLARK, born September, 1858;
died young.

1169. V. CARRIE[6] CLARK, born September 22, 1860;
married C. B. Batchelor, of Pittsfield, N. H.;
had:

1170. I. BERTHA[7] BATCHELOR.

a. XIII. ALVIN B.[5] GOODRICH, born May 4,
1830; lives in Haverhill, Mass.; married,
September 28, 1858, Sarah L. Boston, born
April 1, 1838; had:

1171. I. LAURA E.[6] GOODRICH, born June 5, 1860;
died June 30, 1875.

1172. II. LOIS AUGUSTA[6] GOODRICH, born August
21, 1862; died September 26, 1863.

1173. III. EDWARD EVERETT[6] GOODRICH, born December 1, 1867; died August 4, 1868.

1174. IV. WALTER EVERETT[6] GOODRICH, born December 18, 1871.

1175.   XIV. ANDREW J.[5] GOODRICH, born in Lebanon, September 14, 1832; married, February 24, 1861, Susan A. Whiting. She was born August 10, 1834, in Weymouth, Mass.; had:

1176.   I. JEMIMA MARIA[6] GOODRICH, born December 24, 1861 ; died August 3, 1880.

1177.   II. JOHN J.[6] GOODRICH, born May 29, 1864; married Agatha M. Webster; had :

1178.   I. HERBERT T. A.[7] GOODRICH, born October 3, 1882.

1179.   III. LOIS MABEL[6] GOODRICH, born November 6, 1872.

1180.   XV. JOSEPH F.[5] GOODRICH.

He is an extensive manufacturer of carriages in New Haven, Conn., and merchant in New York City; married Carrie A. Hall.

57.

ELIZABETH[4] BUTLER, third child of Thomas[3] and Bridget (Gerrish) Butler, baptized January 6, 1760 ; married, May 18, 1780, William Chadwick, Jr. Wentworth says that " he was born about 1758, and that he was an adopted son; that he moved to Berwick from Somersworth, N. H., and died there." They had (besides others who died young) :

1181.   I. ABRA[5] CHADWICK, born October 9, 1781 ; married February 12, 1807, John Lord, son of Samuel Lord, of Berwick. He was born in Berwick, September 12, 1785; died March 31, 1855; had:

1182. I. SOPHIA[6] LORD, born November 7, 1807; died April 9, 1833; married, December 6, 1829, William Gowen Wentworth; he died December, 1852; had:

1183. I. THOMAS GRAFTON[7] WENTWORTH, born September 9, 1830.

1184. II. CHARLES EDWARD[7] WENTWORTH, born December 22, 1831.

1185. III. WILLIAM GOWEN[7] WENTWORTH, born April 13, 1833; died August 12, 1833.

1186. II. EMILY[6] LORD, married Thurston Libby, of Auburn, Me.; had:

1187. I. EMILY LIBBY, married Frank Simmons, the sculptor; died in Rome, Italy.

1188. II. NANCY[7] LIBBY.

1189. III. ELIZABETH[7] LIBBY.

1190. IV. MARTHA[7] LIBBY.

1191. III. NANCY[6] LORD, lived at home; single.

1192. IV. ELIZABETH[6] LORD; is single.

1193. V. MARTHA[6] LORD; single.

1194. II. IVORY[5] CHADWICK, born January 4, 1784; drowned June 8, 1798.

1195. BETSY[5] CHADWICK, born November 18, 1785; married, first, December 5, 1806, Daniel Wadleigh, of South Berwick, Me.; second, John Whittier, of Athens, Me.

1196. IV. MARY[5] CHADWICK, born October 1, 1787; married Bartholomew Thompson, of South

Berwick. He is dead. She lived childless at Worcester, Mass., with her niece, Mrs. Mary Bond Fletcher.

1197. V. NANCY[5] CHADWICK, born August 7, 1789; married John Bond, of Boston, Mass.; had:

1198. I. ELIZA ANN[6] BOND, born in Boston, October 22, 1817; married in Boston, June 1, 1837, Charles Wentworth, born in Hallowell, Me, September 23, 1809. In June, 1849, he started for California, and was drowned soon after his arrival there. They had (besides two who died young):

1199. I. MARY FLETCHER[7] WENTWORTH, born in Roxbury, Mass., August 7, 1844.

1200. II. MARY[6] BOND, married ——— Fletcher, and lives in Worcester, Mass.

1201. VI. NATHANIEL[5] CHADWICK, born September 5, 1791; married, September, 1813, Charity, daughter of Thomas and Olive (Chadwick) Abbott, and had fourteen children, all of whom are dead excepting

1202. NATHANIEL[6] CHADWICK, who lives in South Berwick.

1203. VII. JOHN[5] CHADWICK, born in South Berwick, September 5, 1793; drowned, December 25, 1813, while in the privateer service in the war with Great Britain.

1204. VIII. THOMAS[5] CHADWICK, born December 21, 1795; married Amy Knox, of Berwick, Me.

1205. IX. Bridget [5] Chadwick, born January 17, 1802; married James Thompson, of South Berwick; he was brother to Bartholomew Thompson, who married her sister Mary.[5] He died October 22, 1870; she died April 8, 1875.

1206. X. William [5] Chadwick, born April 9, 1804; married, first, Asenath Keay, and is living in Dover, N. H., with second wife.

58.

NATHANIEL [4] BUTLER, fourth child of Thomas[3] and Bridget (Gerrish) Butler, born July 5, 1762; died November 25, 1841. Was a selectman for Sanford several times, and a trader in general merchandise. He married Tabatha Joy; had:

1207. I. Moses,[5] born August 21, 1791; died October 9, 1813.

1208. II. Nathaniel,[5] born November 21, 1794; died December 11, 1872; married Joan Keay; born November 15, 1795, and died November 9, 1879. He was chosen selectman of the town several times. They had:

1209. I. Dorcas S.,[6] born August 23, 1818; married, October 3, 1844, Nathan Dorr, a carpenter and builder. They had:

1210. I. Annie Belle [7] Dorr, born November 21, 1845.

1211. II. Lizzie B.[7] Dorr, born March 4, 1852; died September 15, 1852.

1212. III. SYDNEY B.[7] DORR, born September 17, 1857; married Nettie Reed, of Springvale, Me.; had:

1213. I. EDWIN N.[8] DORR, born March 5, 1879.

1214. II. FRANK N.,[6] born June 20, 1820; was for many years deputy-sheriff for York County, Me., and a member of the school board. He married, first, May 28, 1842, Martha W. Libby; had:

1215. I. CLARA,[7] born December 16, 1843; married, June 30, 1866, Seth Dillingham; had:

1216. I. WILLIS IRWIN[8] DILLINGHAM, born September 9, 1868.

1217. II. LAURA LOTTIE[8] DILLINGHAM, born August 30, 1870.

1218. III. PERLEY SETH[8] DILLINGHAM, born October 29, 1872.

1219. IV. CORA[8] DILLINGHAM, born February 12, 1875.

1220. V. PAUL[8] DILLINGHAM, born May 20, 1880.

1221. II. LAURA,[7] born November 8, 1844; married, October 14, 1862, Ansel Chick; had:

1222. I. CARRIE MATTIE[8] CHICK, born February 22, 1864.

1223. II. SARAH ELIZABETH[8] CHICK, born March 4, 1868.

1224. III. VENICE RAY[8] CHICK, born December 5, 1872; died April 20, 1883.

1225. III. ARETHUSA,[7] born June 22, 1846; died

April 9, 1876; married, October 27, 1868, Charles F. Hasty; had:

1226. I. CHARLES L.[8] HASTY, born July 16, 1871; died July 21, 1871.

1227. IV. HARVEY,[7] born March 21, 1848; died February 26, 1854.

1228. V. SARAH GERTRUDE,[7] born December 6, 1849; and a son born December 9, 1851, who died an infant; his wife, Martha (Libby), died November 28, 1853. He married again November 22, 1854, Mary Dorr, and had by her:

1229. VI. HARVEY D.,[7] born November 28, 1857; died February 28, 1883.

1230. VII. ANNIE E.,[7] born September 29, 1860; married, January 1, 1879, Ezekiel H. A. Prescott; had:

1231. I. HARVEY SCOTT[8] PRESCOTT, born January 28, 1880.

1232. II. N. J.[8] PRESCOTT, born September 5, 1882.

1233. III. S. ELIZABETH,[6] born April 4, 1823; died 1847.

1234. IV. ANN,[6] born June 14, 1828; died 1852; married, 1850, Judge Hanscomb, of St. Paul, Minn., formerly a lawyer of China, Me.; had:

1235. I. ANNIE B.[7] HANSCOMB; she married Henry Rice.

1236. V. JAMES S.,[6] born August 12, 1832; died 1862.

1237. VI. B. Franklin,[6] born September 2, 1837; died 1838.

1238. III. Mehitable,[5] born October 3, 1796; died September 16, 1870; married Elias Libby, of Berwick; had :

1239. I. Mary[6] Libby, born in Sanford, Me., February 8, 1819; married, 1840, Benjamin F. Hanson.

1240. II. Tabatha[6] Libby, born August 13, 1821; is single.

1241. III. Asenath[6] Libby, born February 24, 1823; married Rosina Libby.

1242. IV. Luther Samuel[6] Libby, born February 28, 1825.

1243. V. Susan[6] Libby, born February 11, 1828.

1244. VI. Nathaniel B.[6] Libby, born December 4, 1832; married Susan Jane Libby, and lives in Orleans, Ia.

1245. VII. John Howard[6] Libby, born June 8, 1835; died March 31, 1836.

1246. VIII. Elias H.[6] Libby, born October 26, 1837.

1247. IX. Mehitable Josephine[6] Libby, born January 8, 1841; married William Howard Hill, of Sanford, Me.

1248. IV. Bridget,[5] born January 7, 1799; died June 18, 1826; married Hawley Keay; had :

1249. I. Nathaniel Washburne[6] Keay, born in Sanford, June 18, 1822; died in Bolivia, South America, May, 1880.

1250. II. CYRUS PROCTOR KEAY, born August 20, 1824.

1251. III. BRIDGET KEAY, born June 1, 1826; died October 13, 1832.

1252. V. NEHEMIAH,[5] born April 14, 1801; died April 8, 1877. He lived in Sanford, and was a Representative in the State Legislature during several terms, and held other offices of the town. He married, 1824, Aphia Libby; she was born March 15, 1803; died April 6, 1843; they had:

1253. I. LEWIS,[6] born in Sanford, December 15, 1824; married, September 5, 1855, Hannah J. Tibbitts; had:

1254. I. LEWIS.[7]

1255. II. ADAH,[6] born November 10, 1826; married, March 8, 1851, John B.[6] Libby (1255), son of Susan[5] (1254) (Butler) and Ebenezer Libby; he was born in Sanford, November 10, 1824, whom see for children.

1256. III. DENNIS,[6] born August 21, 1828; died October 26, 1858; married, February 22, 1856, Frances F. Guptill; had:

1257. I. ARTHUR D.,[7] born December 7, 1857; married, August 20, 1879, Melvina E. Nason.

1258. II. NATHANIEL,[7] born June 8, 1859; died single.

1259. IV. EMILY A.,[6] born November 9, 1830; married, May 30, 1857, George W. Pray; had:

9

1260. I. ALICE J.[7] PRAY, born in Sanford, August 10, 1858; died April 15, 1881.

1261. II. CHARLES A.[7] PRAY, born November 17, 1860.

1262. III. GEORGE F.[7] PRAY, born May 30, 1868; died July 1, 1868.

1263. IV. EVA LAURA[7] PRAY, born August 22, 1870; died May 10, 1871.

1264. V. G. WILLIAM[7] PRAY, born April 12, 1873.

1265. V. LAVINIA,[6] born August 8, 1833.

1266. VI. DRAXCY,[6] born October 26, 1835; married, February 26, 1856, Horace M. Ford; had:

1267. I. MYRA A.[7] FORD, born May 26, 1857; died September 4, 1858.

1268. II. NEHEMIAH B.[7] FORD, born in Boston, Mass., October 2, 1863.

1269. VII. NATHANIEL,[6] born March 30, 1838; died October 6, 1858.

1270. VIII. LEBBIUS,[6] born February 3, 1841; married, November 29, 1866, Olive O. Ford; had:

1271. I. HARVEY A.,[7] born April 3, 1872.

1272. II. AUBREY O.,[7] born March 23, 1874.

NEHEMIAH[5] (1231), married again, April, 1844, Rhoda Chadbourne; had by her:

1273. IX. APHIA,[6] born May 15, 1845; married, January 17, 1863, Ivory H. Ford.

1274. X. ROXILLA,[6] born November 22, 1847; died January 10, 1851.

1275. XI. ROXILLA, again, born December 15, 1851.

1276. VI. SUSAN,[5] born April 4, 1803; married, first, Ebenezer Libby, brother of Elias, who married her sister Mehitable[5]; second, William Chadbourne, of Sanford. She had all by first husband.

1277. I. JOHN B.[6] LIBBY, born November 10, 1824. He was one of the board of selectmen of Sanford; married, March 8, 1851, Adah[6] (1233), daughter of Nehemiah[5] (1231) and Aphia (Libby) Butler; had:

1278. I. EMMA ROSINA[7] LIBBY, born March 11, 1856; is single.

1279. II. EBEN HERBERT[7] LIBBY, born June 1, 1860.

1280. III. CHARLES IRVING[7] LIBBY, born August 11, 1862.

1281. IV. JOHN HAVEN[7] LIBBY, born October 25, 1864.

1282. V. PAREPA ROSA[7] LIBBY, born August 26, 1867.

1283. VI. LEWIS BUTLER[7] LIBBY, born June 8, 1869.

1284. II. MOSES HEBRON[6] LIBBY, born in Sanford, October 5, 1826. He has always lived on his father's homestead; has been one of the selectmen of Sanford for several terms; married, February 5, 1850, Martha Moulton, of Sanford; had:

1285. I. ORVILLE VINTON[7] LIBBY, born March 21,

1851; married first, October 14, 1876, Susan
A. Bennett. She died April 18, 1878 ; married again, November 14, 1880, Abbie J.
Shaw.

1286. II. Susan Annette[7] Libby, born September
11, 1852; married, 1877, Charles A. Bodwell.

1287. III. Martha Francina[7] Libby, born June
26, 1854; married Theodore B. Hobbs.

1288. IV. Moses Hebron[7] Libby, born April 17,
1858.

1289. V. Ida May[7] Libby, born July 23, 1861 ;
married, February 1, 1879, Frank H. Gerrish.

1290. VI. Loren Wirtie[7] Libby, born November
17, 1867; died February 24, 1873.

1291. VII. Lillian Iona[7] Libby, born with Loren
W., November 17, 1867.

1292. VIII. Ella Moulton[7] Libby, born February
2, 1870.

1293. IX. Fred. Loren[7] Libby, born April 8,
1875.

1294. III. Rowena[6] Libby, born January 23, 1829 ;
married Luther Libby.

1295. IV. Ada Ann[6] Libby, born April 28, 1831 ;
married, February 10, 1863, William F.
Johnson, of Sanford, and is dead.

1296. V. Ivory Ashton[6] Libby, born September 1,
1833; married, March 8, 1858, Beulah A.
Stevens, of Great Falls, N. H., and lives in
Iowa; had:

1297. I. Viola I.[7] Libby, born December 29, 1859; died March 31, 1881; married, April 3, 1878, Henry W. Potter.

1298. II. Dora M.[7] Libby, born April 3, 1860; married, December 3, 1879, John Walton.

1299. III. Milton O.[7] Libby, born December 28, 1861.

1300. IV. Flora E.[7] Libby, born April 28, 1865.

1301. V. Frank E.[7] Libby, born March 17, 1867.

1302. VI. Fred O.[7] Libby, born February 2, 1869; died March 12, 1874.

1303. VII. Ivory H.[7] Libby, born March 18, 1870; died October 6, 1870.

1304. VIII. Minnie A.[7] Libby, born June 21, 1874.

1305. IX. Walter R.[7] Libby, born November 24, 1876.

1306. VI. Eben H.[6] Libby, born May 12, 1836; died November 16, 1855.

1307. VII. Susan J.[6] Libby, born May 15, 1838; married her cousin, Nathaniel Libby.

1308. VIII. Tabatha Angeline[6] Libby, born August 5, 1840; married, January, 1867, Oscar C. Cole, of Fayette, Fayette County, Ia.; has been editor of the *Volga Valley Times.*

1309. VII. John,[5] born August 1, 1805; died September 7, 1806.

1310. VIII. Mary,[5] born June 30, 1807; married August 16, 1829, Deacon Ivory Libby, brother of Elias, who married her sister Mehitable,[5] and of Ebenezer, who married

her Sister Susan, and of Aphia and Rhoda,
who married her brother Nehemiah.[5]   They
live in Berwick, and had:

1311. I. JULIA A.[6] LIBBY, born January 16, 1830;
married, March 7, 1850, Richard M. Ellsworth; had:

1312. I. LAURA EMMA[7] ELLSWORTH, born November
15, 1852; married, March 30, 1872, Charles
Howard; had:

1313. I. BLANCHE[8] HOWARD, born November 4,
1877.

1314. II. FRED[7] ELLSWORTH, born September 6,
1855; married, March 4, 1881, Carrie E. Ja-
cobs; had:

1315. I. LEE EARL[8] ELLSWORTH, born July 4, 1883.

1316. II. ERNEST[8] ELLSWORTH, born July 3, 1884;
died young.

1317. III. JULIA E.[7] ELLSWORTH, born February 5,
1863.

1318. II. PHILANDER H.[6] LIBBY, born December 18,
1831; married Mary A. Lougee; had:

1319. I. HENRY W.[7] LIBBY, born May 16, 1858;
died December 21, 1879.

1320. II. ELMER E.[7] LIBBY, born September 19,
1861.

1321. III. FRED[7] LIBBY, born 1863.

1322. IV. ARABELLA L.[7] LIBBY, born May 17, 1865.

1323. V. MAUDE S.[7] LIBBY, born August 8, 1867.

1324. VI. JOHN T.[7] LIBBY, born September 1, 1875;
died young.

1325. VII. JESSIE I.[7] LIBBY, born August 7, 1879.

1326. III. MAY J.[6] LIBBY, born February 3, 1834 ; died October 6, 1876.

1327. IV. RHODA A.[6] LIBBY, born May 24, 1836 ; married, October 13, 1864, Daniel Toothaker, of Phillips, Me. ; had :

1328. I. CORA A.[7] TOOTHAKER, born September 26, 1865.

1329. II. IVORY N.[7] TOOTHAKER, born May 26, 1867 ; died October 4, 1873.

1330. III. NETTIE LULU[7] TOOTHAKER, born February 10, 1875.

1331. IV. GRACE EDNA[7] TOOTHAKER, born December 18, 1878.

1332. V. IVORY BUTLER[6] LIBBY, born March 31, 1839 ; went to California in 1857.

1333. VI. GILBERT N.[6] LIBBY, born March 19, 1842 ; married, July 11, 1872, Belle McNebo, in Prairie-du-Chien ; had (besides one son died young) :

1334. I. MABEL B.[7] LIBBY, born March 9, 1875.

1335. II. CORA BELLE[7] LIBBY, born March 15, 1878 ; died July 4, 1878.

1336. VII. APHIA[6] LIBBY, born February 19, 1844 ; died February 17, 1870.

1337. VIII. MOSES A.[6] LIBBY, born July 5, 1848.

1338. IX. TABATHA,[5] born December 19, 1810 ; died April 24, 1865 ; married, 1857, Sheldon Beal ; he died January 10, 1875 ; had :

1339. I. NATHANIEL BUTLER[6] BEAL, born March 7,

1828; married April 8, 1849, Mary Robbins; had:

1340. I. FRED MARSHALL[7] BEAL, born April 24, 1855; died January 12, 1857.

1341. II. MINNIE GENEVRA[7] BEAL, born May 20, 1858; married, June 28, 1880, James Watson Smith.

1342. III. FRED NATHANIEL[7] BEAL, born April 14, 1860; married, March 1, 1885, Ella Harvey.

1343. II. WILLIAM C.[6] BEAL, born May 8, 1830; married June 8, 1860, Mary Wells; had:

1344. I. LINDA ALTHEA[7] BEAL, born April 21, 1862.

1345. II. HELEN MARIA[7] BEAL, born July 28, 1866.

1346. III. CARRIE ELVIRA[7] BEAL, born August 28, 1869.

1347. IV. IDA MAY[7] BEAL, born September 25, 1876.

1348. III. HORACE[6] BEAL, born March 13, 1832; married, November 5, 1860, Elvira Horn; had:

1349. I. MINNIE A.[7] BEAL, born May 3, 1862.

1350. II. SHELDON HOBBS[7] BEAL, born February 7, 1864.

1351. IV. LEWIS[6] BEAL, born June 13, 1834; married, June 13, 1863, Althea Mitchell; had:

1352. I. ALVENO A.[7] BEAL, born March 8, 1864.

1353. II. LEON LEWIS[7] BEAL, born March 13, 1868.

1354. III. BERTHA LEE[7] BEAL, born March 8, 1870.

1355. IV. PERLEY BRADFORD[7] BEAL, born March 13, 1874.

1356. V. Bradford[6] Beal, born August 4, 1836; married, July 23, 1865, Abbie Lambert; had:

1357. I. Marcia Lena[7] Beal, born August 1, 1867.

1358. II. Samuel Lambert[7] Beal, born November 15, 1870.

1359. VI. Sheldon[6] Beal, born July 12, 1839; died June 17, 1864.

1360. VII. Laura[6] Beal, born January 5, 1842; married first, December 19, 1863, William Grafton Bradbury. He died March 16, 1866; had:

1361. I. Sheldon Hobbs[7] Bradbury, born June 25, 1864.

1362. II. William W.[7] Bradbury, born with Sheldon H., June 25, 1864.

She married again, August 8, 1871, Joseph Pollard Adams.

1363. VIII. Valora[6] Beal, born November 8, 1849; married, November 8, 1866, Eastman Jason Ross; had:

1364. I. Margie Lena[7] Ross, born August 11, 1873.

1365. II. M. V.[7] Ross, born September 19, 1879.

1366. III. Lee Eastman J.[7] Ross, born March 31, 1881.

1367. IX. Eldora[6] Beal, born July 9, 1851; married, January 22, 1873, Alvin J. Goodwin; had:

1368. I. Harry Horner[7] Goodwin, born May 25, 1874.

1369. X. Moses,[5] born January 10, 1814; died
        September 12, 1853; married Philena John-
        son; had:
1370. I. Roxana,[6] born January 13, 1841; married
        Allen T. Worcester, of Lebanon, Me.; had:
1371. I. Frank V.[7] Worcester, born in Great
        Falls, N. H., April, 1885.
1372. II. Nathaniel H.,[6] born June 13, 1842; mar-
        ried, 1878, Jennie Moore, and lives in New
        York.
1373. III. Marion Adelaide,[6] born March 4, 1846;
        married William B. Gowen; had:
1374. I. Madelon Maria[7] Gowen.

59.

THOMAS[4] BUTLER, fifth child of Thomas[3] and
    Bridget (Gerrish) Butler, baptized June 19, 1763;
    married Olive Abbott, and lived in Limerick,
    Me.; had:
1375. I. George.[5]
1376. II. Hannah.[5]
1377. III. Oliver.[5]

60.

MARY[4] BUTLER, sixth child of Thomas[3] and
    Bridget (Gerrish) Butler; married, first, May 8,
    1788, Isaac Gerrish, Jr.; second, —— Cunning-
    ham; no issue.

61.

SARAH[4] BUTLER, daughter of Thomas[3] and
Bridget (Gerrish) Butler; married, April 17,
1790, Stephen Libby, of Berwick, Me. He was
born April 12, 1764; died October 19, 1833. She
died December, 1851; had:

1378. I. NATHANIEL[5] LIBBY, born in Shapleigh,
April 19, 1791; married, September 14, 1815,
Anna Ricker. He died June 24, 1857. She
died July 30, 1849. They had:

1379. I. DAVID[6] LIBBY, born January 6, 1816;
married in Boston, Sarah[5] (1466), daughter
of William[4] and Lois (Littlefield) Butler,
born January 13, 1819. He died April 25,
1857, in Kennebunkport; for children see
descendants of William[4] and Lois Butler.

1380. II. (DEACON) AARON[6] LIBBY, born February
5, 1818; married Rosina Jaqueth or Jaffrey,
N. H.; had:

1381. I. LEWIS NATHANIEL[7] LIBBY, born January
23, 1846; married, May 8, 1870, Aurania,
daughter of Rev. William A. Sargent, of
Vineland, N. J. He died November, 1870,
in Kennebunkport; had:

1382. I. LEWIS WAYLAND[8] LIBBY, born after the
death of his father.

1383. II. CHARLES CHESTER[7] LIBBY, born April 10,
1849.

1384. III. EDMOND DORNAM[7] LIBBY, born November 1, 1851. He graduated at Dartmouth College in the class of 1879.

1385. IV. WILLIE HOWARD[7] LIBBY, born January 15, 1855.

1386. V. LIZZIE ANNA[7] LIBBY, born August 7, 1857; married, October, 1876, Daniel Cleaves.

1387. III. LAVINIA[6] LIBBY, born March 28, 1820; married, January 24, 1843, B. F. Baker, of Brookline, Mass.

1388. IV. STEPHEN[6] LIBBY, born November 1, 1825; died October 8, 1866; single.

1389. V. NATHANIEL LEWIS[6] LIBBY, born November 1, 1825; died October 13, 1832.

1390. VI. ELIZABETH ANN[6] LIBBY, born November 17, 1829.

1391. II. NANCY GERRISH[6] LIBBY, born April 22, 1793; married, February 27, 1817, Captain John Cook Libby; had:

1392. I. SALLY[6] LIBBY, born February 16, 1818; married, December 25, 1849, James Johnson.

1393. II. ASA[6] LIBBY, born August 19, 1820; married, June, 1852, Lydia Lord, of Limington; had:

1394. I. CHARLES HERBERT[7] LIBBY, born June 27, 1853; married, September, 1878, Annie M., daughter of William Johnson, of Parsonsfield; had:

1395. I. JOSEPHINE H.[8] LIBBY, born in Denver, Col., March 21, 1880.

1396. II. EMMA JANE[7] LIBBY, born February 22,

1855; married, October 2, 1877, George E. Tuxbury, of Saco, Me.

1397. III. MARY ABBIE [7] LIBBY, born February 26, 1857.

1398. IV. JOHN WILBUR [7] LIBBY, born August 9, 1859.

1399. V. NANCY ALICE [7] LIBBY, born March 5, 1861.

1400. VI. ALBERT ELLSWORTH [7] LIBBY, born February 20, 1863.

1401. VII. EUGENE ASA [7] LIBBY, born July 26, 1867.

1402. VIII. ANNIE CELIA [7] LIBBY, born January 30, 1870.

1403. III. STEPHEN COOK [6] LIBBY, M.D., born April 1, 1822; married, June 27, 1852, Sarah A., daughter of James and Nancy (Davis) Frost, of Limington. He graduated from the Worcester Medical College of Massachusetts, is a physician and druggist in Saco. He has served in both branches of the city government, and in 1874 was Republican candidate for Mayor; they had:

1404. I. ELWIN [7] LIBBY, born July 10, 1856; died August 10, 1856.

1405. II. CARRIE EMMA [7] LIBBY, born September 28, 1857; died January 20, 1878.

1406. III. FRANK HOWARD [7] LIBBY, born November 4, 1862.

1407. IV. ELLA FROST [7] LIBBY, born September 30, 1866.

1408. IV. John [6] Libby, born February 6, 1826; married Hannah Edgerly, of Exeter, N. H. He died July 30, 1860. She died about 1874.

1409. V. Samuel Jackson [6] Libby, born June 17, 1830; died July, 1854. Was a schoolmaster.

1410. VI. Ann [6] Libby, born July 16, 1831; married Alfred Mitchell, of Lewiston, Me.

1411. VII. Silea [6] Libby, born February 1, 1835; married, December 23, 1855, Charles F. Baker.

1412. III. Bridget [5] Libby, born in Sanford, December 7, 1794; married, March 23, 1819, Nathaniel Ricker.

1413. IV. Lavinia [5] Libby, born in Limerick, Me., December 29, 1796; married, October 9, 1833, Paul Hussey.

1414. V. Silea [5] Libby, born in Limerick, Me., March 3, 1799; married, January 1, 1822, Hiram Joy.

1415. VI. Stephen [5] Libby, born in Limerick, November 20, 1801; married, first, Nancy Libby; again, Mary Jane Bradeen; had all by first wife:

1416. I. William Wallace [6] Libby, born November 30, 1836; married, May 17, 1868, Abbie F., daughter of Samuel and Sally (Goodwin) Lougee, of Parsonsfield, Me.; had:

1417. I. Louis Clifford [7] Libby, born in Waterborough, Me., March 10, 1869.

1418. II. GERTRUDE CLARE [7] LIBBY, born May 24, 1874.

1419. III. EDNA INES [7] LIBBY, born January 12, 1877; died November 6, 1879.

1420. II. ROSALTHEA [6] LIBBY, born March 31, 1839; married Silas C. Robbins, of Phillips, Me.

1421. III. Rev. CHARLES LORING [6] LIBBY, born January 21, 1844; married, January 27, 1867, in Anoka, Minn., Emma A., daughter of Samuel and Cordelia (Hill) Richardson, of Limington, Me. He is pastor of the M. E. Church in Denver, Col. They had:

1422. I. NELLIE [7] LIBBY, born in Grow, Minn., October 3, 1868.

1423. II. FRED L. [7] LIBBY, born in Anoka, Minn., August 26, 1870.

1424. III. HENRY P. [7] LIBBY, born in Anoka, September 20, 1872.

1425. IV. ROLLA [7] LIBBY, born in Atwater, Minn., April 12, 1876.

a. IV. MARY ALICE [6] LIBBY, born June 14, 1850; married James Everett Chandler, of Biddeford, Me.

1426. VII. WILLIAM [5] LIBBY, born September 21, and died September 30, 1802.

1427. VIII. CYRUS [5] LIBBY, born in Limerick, Me., January 24, 1804; married, November 4, 1829, Drusilla, daughter of William and Theodosia (Thompson) Woodsom, of Waterborough; had (all born in Limerick, Me.):

1428. I. SILEA[6] LIBBY, born April 11, 1825; died August 31, 1828.

1429. II. MELISSA[6] LIBBY, born March 3, 1827; died September 28, 1841.

1430. III. CYRUS[6] LIBBY, born January 1, 1830; married, February 13, 1859, Lavinia L., daughter of Obed and Sarah W. (Lock) Varney, of Rochester, N. H.; had:

1431. I. CHARLES EDWARD[7] LIBBY, born February 13, 1861.

1432. II. SARAH WINSLOW[7] LIBBY, born April 14, 1863.

1433. III. LAVINIA EMMA[7] LIBBY, born June 30, 1866.

1434. IV. CYRUS OSGOOD[7] LIBBY, born April 27, 1871.

1435. IV. SARAH E.[6] LIBBY, born December 5, 1831; married, October 10, 1852, Charles A. Whipp.

1436. V. CATHERINE M.[6] LIBBY, born October 5, 1833; married, May 31, 1854, Isaac T. Storer.

1437. VI. WILLIAM[6] LIBBY, died in early childhood.

1438. VII. STEPHEN[6] LIBBY, died young.

1439. VIII. SUSAN[6] LIBBY, born December 29, 1838; married, first, Mark Thwing; again, George Gayman, of Dedham, Mass.

1440. IX. STEPHEN[6] LIBBY, born December 19, 1839; married, August 27, 1872, Abbie O., daughter of George and Sally (Moulton) Moore, of Newfield, Me.

1441. X. WILLIAM OSBORN[6] LIBBY, born October 29, 1841; married ——— McKusick.

1442. XI. LAMEN COLBY[6] LIBBY, born October 17, 1844; lives in South Boston.

1443. IX. ROOK THURSTON[5] LIBBY, born in Limerick, Me., January 27, 1806; married, first, December 28, 1831, Emily, daughter of John and Abra (Chadwick) Lord, of Somersworth, N. H. She died June 25, 1851, in Saco. Second, Marion Bradbury, of Hollis, Me. She died October, 1861. He married again, Martha J. Wyman. He owned and operated mills on Little Ossipee River, and in Hollis and Saco. He had by first wife Emily:

1444. I. MARY[6] LIBBY, born October 27, 1832; died June 12, 1855.

1445. II. IVORY EMERSON[6] LIBBY, born September 7, 1834; married, November 3, 1859, Lucinda, daughter of James and Nancy (Stevens) Leavitt, of Waterborough; died November, 1866; had two children who died in infancy.

1446. III. LUCINDA[6] LIBBY, born February 13, 1836; died May 17, 1862.

1447. IV. EMILY J.[6] LIBBY, born November 21, 1837; married Frank Simmons, the sculptor; died September 18, 1871, in Rome, Italy.

1448. V. GEORGE[6] LIBBY, born January 16, 1840; died in infancy.

10

1449. VI. MARTHA[6] LIBBY, born February 25, 1842; died young.

1450. VII. GEORGE [6] LIBBY, born January 25, 1845; died September 2, 1846.

1451. VIII. CHARLES H.[6] LIBBY, born November 1, 1846; died January 9, 1858.

1452. IX. HARRIET A.[6] LIBBY, born March 26, 1849; died June 12, 1861.

By second wife, Marion:

1453. X. ELSIE ELLA [6] LIBBY, born March 10, 1852; married, March 2, 1874, James Hamilton, of Harrison.

1454. XI. IDA M.[6] LIBBY, born in 1857; died June 4, 1864.

1455. XII. JENNIE T.[6] LIBBY, died December 28, 1861.

1456. X. THOMAS BUTLER [5] LIBBY, born in Limerick, December 9, 1808; married, March 20, 1834, his cousin, Eunice[5] (1478), daughter of William [4] (67) and Lois (Littlefield) Butler, of Sanford. He lived on his father's homestead and died June 8, 1842. She married again February 4, 1844, Walter H. Pierce, of Limerick, and still occupies the homestead. For children, see 1478 in descendants of William [4] and Lois (Littlefield).

1457. XI. ALICE [5] LIBBY, born May 22, 1810; died August 2, 1850; single.

1458. XII. MARY [5] LIBBY, born April 4, 1815; died August 13, 1852.

63.

HANNAH[4] BUTLER, daughter of Thomas[3] and Bridget (Gerrish) Butler; married Barnabas Sawyer, and lived in Buxton, Me.

64.

BRIDGET[4] BUTLER, daughter of Thomas[3] and Bridget (Gerrish) Butler; married, March 12, 1792, William Heard.

65.

MERCY[4] BUTLER, daughter of Thomas[3] and Bridget (Gerrish) Butler; married Jacob Stone. Lived in Sanford.

66.

SUSAN[4] BUTLER, daughter of Thomas[3] and Bridget (Gerrish) Butler; married, first, Rook Thurston, of Wells (certificate granted February 24, 1800); second, Stephen (Samuel?) Edgerly; had :

1459. I. STEPHEN[5] EDGERLY.
1460. II. ROOK[5] EDGERLY.
1461. III. SARAH[5] EDGERLY.
1462. IV. MARY[5] EDGERLY.

67.

WILLIAM [4] BUTLER, youngest child of Thomas [3] and Bridget (Gerrish) Butler; married, August 27, 1803 (certificate granted August 16, 1803, in Sanford), Lois Littlefield. He died March 20, 1838. They had:

1463. I. CYRUS,[5] born February 9, 1804; died young.

1464. II. MARY,[5] born October 21, 1805; married Edmond Brown; had:

1465. I. WILLIAM H.[6] BROWN.

1466. II. THOMAS [6] BROWN, and others.

1467. III. THOMAS,[5] born March 27, 1807; died in Connecticut.

1468. IV. WLLIAM,[5] born June 24, 1808; married and lived in Connecticut.

1469. V. ASENATH,[5] born June 2, 1810; died young.

1470. VI. CYRUS,[5] (again) born October 23, 1811.

1471. VII. SALLY,[5] born with Cyrus, October 23, 1811; married Cyrus Libby, of North Waterborough, Me.

1472. VIII. STEPHEN,[5] born November 27, 1812; married, first, Elizabeth Furber; again, Adelaide Hodsdon, of Winstead, Conn.; had, by first wife, Elizabeth:

1473. I. AMOS.[6]

1474. II. WILLIAM.[6]

1475. IX. AMOS H.,[5] born March 25, 1814; married, September 30, 1839, Rebecca Stenman; had :

1476. I. WILLIAM VAN BUREN,[6] born August 9, 1840 ; died March, 1865.

1477. II. AMOS FRANKLIN,[6] died January, 1843.

1478. X. EUNICE,[5] born in Sanford, September 25, 1815; married, March 20, 1834, Thomas[5] Butler Libby (1456), son of Sarah,[4] (61) daughter of Thomas[3] (24) and Bridget (Gerrish) Butler; again, Walter Pierce, of Limerick; had by first husband:

1479. I. ALMEDA J.[6] LIBBY, born December 9, 1834; married, January 10, 1859, William Abbott Lang, of Limerick.

1480. II. LOIS B.[6] LIBBY, born February 25, 1836; married, May 5, 1857, Elisha Wadleigh, of Parsonsfield.

1481. III. MARTIN VAN BUREN[6] LIBBY, born June 20, 1837; was a mariner; left home for a voyage at sea and never afterward heard from.

1482. IV. STEPHEN FRANK[6] LIBBY (known as Frank S.), born March 26, 1840; married June 16, 1863, Sarah J., daughter of John and Nancy (Davis) Fisk, of Waterborough, widow of Daniel C. Warren; had :

1483. I. ELLSWORTH LINCOLN[7] LIBBY, born June 12, 1865.

1484. II. EDWARD EVERETT[7] LIBBY, born July 27, 1867.

1485. III. WARREN SUMNER [7] LIBBY, born June 11, 1871.

1486. V. BUTLER [6] LIBBY, born February 6, 1842; married, December 19, 1863, Sarah E., daughter of John and Sarah Ann (Harper) Brooks, of Limerick, Me. During the War of the Rebellion, he served three years in the 11th Massachusetts Light Artillery. He is in business as the Cable Lightning Rod Co., and has been Republican candidate for Representative in the State Legislature; had:

1487. I. JOHN HARVEY BURNSIDE [7] LIBBY, born September 15, 1864.

1488. II. LILLIAN M. [7] LIBBY, born in East Cambridge, Mass., March 20, 1867.

1489. XI. LOIS, [5] born January 1, 1817.

1490. XII. SARAH, [5] born January 13, 1819; married David [6] Libby (1379). He was born January 6, 1816; had:

1491. I. HELEN [7] LIBBY, died an infant.

1492. II. ANSEL [7] LIBBY, lives in Dedham, Mass.

1493. XIII. TABITHA, [5] born July 21, 1820; married ――― Talbot.

1494. XIV. BRIDGET, [5] born February 19, 1822; married ――― Beal, and lives in Springvale, Me.

1495. XV. SUSANNAH, [5] born August 23, 1823.

1496. XVI. ELIZABETH, [5] born November 13, 1825.

69.

JOSEPH[4] BUTLER, second child of Charles[3] and Sarah (Cross) Butler, born in South Berwick, Me., January 16, 1761; died May 8, 1826; married, January 8, 1795, Mary Lydston, of Eliot, Me. She died February 2, 1841. He was one of the early settlers of Sanford, Me. Moved there in 1795; had:

1497. I. JOHN,[5] born in Sanford, December 12, 1795; died December 14, 1795.

1498. II. SARAH,[5] born in Sanford, March 12, 1797; died October 20, 1814.

1499. III. LYDIA,[5] born in Sanford, February 5, 1799; married, November 8, 1827, John Hill, of Sanford. She died October 20, 1840, and he soon afterward; they had:

1500. I. JOHN[6] HILL, born in Sanford.

1501. II. S. B.[6] HILL, born in Sanford; is married and had children.

1502. IV. JAMES,[5] born in Sanford, September 5, 1801; died April 20, 1844; married, October 7, 1824, Susan Heard. She died July 22, 1846; they had:

1503. I. JOSEPH,[6] born in Sanford, March 24, 1826; married, June, 1853, Alma Mott, of Great Falls, N. H. He died November 11, 1859; they had:

1504. I. ELLA S.[7] MOTT, born June, 1855; married, August 5, 1877, James Otis Bradbury.

1505. II. IRVING A.,[6] born in Sanford, March 30, 1828; married, June 22, 1859, Martha A. Merrill, and is a manufacturer in Springvale, Me. They had (besides one who died young):

1506. I. BERTHA M.,[7] born in Sanford, May 15, 1865.

1507. III. SARAH,[6] born September 19, 1829; is single.

1508. IV. JOHN N.,[6] born in Sanford, May 5, 1831; died January 6, 1867; married May, 1864, Mary E. Hodsdon; had:

1509. I. ERNEST N.,[7] born March 18, 1866.

1510. V. SUSAN E.,[6] born in Sanford, December 11, 1832; died May 21, 1837.

1511. VI. JAMES W.,[6] born in Sanford, December 21, 1835; married, October 6, 1872, Mary J. Cheney; no issue.

1512. VII. FERDINAND A.,[6] born in Sanford, December 15, 1837; married, May 13, 1875, Jennie M. Giles, of Shapleigh, Me. He died August 19, 1838; they had:

1513. I. ELMON F.,[7] born in Sanford, June 12, 1877.

71.

MOSES[4] BUTLER, fourth child of Charles[3] and Sarah (Cross) Butler, born in Berwick, January 21, 1766; married, first, in Sanford, Abigail Pugsley; she died January 21, 1810. He married again, Mary Pray, born April 22, 1788;

died March 20, 1877. He died July 18, 1850.
He had, by first wife:

1514. I. Annie,[5] born February 5, 1798; died September, 1873; married Captain Nathan Goodwin, of Sanford, a soldier in the war of 1812; had:

1515. I. Sarah[6] Goodwin, born August 25, 1818; died young.

1516. II. Abigail[6] Goodwin, born November 20, 1819; died young.

1517. III. Stephen[6] Goodwin, born June 10, 1821.

1518. IV. Mahala[6] Goodwin, born April 27, 1823; died December 6, 1857.

1519. V. Nathan[6] Goodwin, born June 22, 1825; died young.

1520. VI. William[6] Goodwin, born December 31, 1826.

1521. VII. Ann[6] Goodwin, born May 4, 1828; died 1848.

1522. VIII. Sarah[6] Goodwin, born August 29, 1830; married, September 24, 1858. Joseph Scott, at Rochester, N. H.; had:

1523. I. Nathan H.[7] Scott, born March 14, 1861; died May 29, 1869.

1524. II. Anna B.[7] Scott, born August 30, 1862; died young.

1525. III. Jane E.[7] Scott, born February 13, 1865.

1526. IV. William B.[7] Scott, born July 27, 1868.

1527. II. Sarah,[5] born in Sanford, July 28, 1799;

married August 15, 1830, David Marsh, of
Sanford. She died June 4, 1857. He mar-
ried, again, her sister Love [5] (Butler) (1577)
Hubbard. Sarah had:

1528. I. ELIZABETH [6] MARSH, born June 22, 1831;
married, June 17, 1848, William M.[6] Pray
(674), of Boston, Mass., son of James and
Mary [3] (673) (Butler) Pray, of Lebanon,
Me.; had:

1529. I. FRANK [7] PRAY, born November 11, 1849;
died young.

1530. II. CARRIE A.[7] PRAY, born March 5, 1851;
married, Emerson (William [7]) Miller, November 6, 1872; had:

1531. I. FRED S.[8] MILLER, born March 25, 1875.

1532. III. FRANK W.[7] PRAY, born July 5, 1855;
died young.

1533. IV. EFFIE [7] PRAY, born July 9, 1856.

1534. II. ASBURY C.[6] MARSH, born September, 1833.

1535. III. HENRY B.[6] MARSH, born September,
1835; died young.

1536. III. JOHN B.,[5] born in Sanford, January 2,
1801; married, first, July, 1826, Lucinda
Hurd; second, 1874, Susan Butler; died
1877; third, Mrs. Susan Davis, of Shapleigh; and lived in Sanford, Me.; had, all by
first wife:

1537. I. JAMES S.,[6] born in Sanford, December 30,
1827; married Hannah Kimball, of Newburyport, Mass.; resides in Salem.

1538. II. FRANCIS H.,[6] born in Sanford, September 12, 1832; died October 24, 1872; married Lorinda Ricker, of Great Falls, N. H.

1539. III. OLIVE A.,[6] born in Sanford, April 25, 1834: single.

1540. IV. CHARLES E.,[6] born April 9, 1836: married, May 29, 1856, Mary E., daughter of the late Rev. Joseph Gilpatrick, of Shapleigh; had:

1541. I. PERLEY J.,[7] born October 21, 1857.

1542. II. FRED E.,[7] born January 3, 1863.

1543. III. LESLIE J.,[7] born March 18, 1865.

1544. IV. WILLIS H.,[7] born June 27, 1867; died November 11, 1881.

1545. V. JOHN F.,[6] born in Sanford, December 28, 1838; married Abbie[6] Ricker (618), daughter of Ebenezer[5] (601) and Susan[5] (Butler) (773) Ricker, of Lebanon; had:

1546. I. J. EBENEZER,[7] born June 26, 1862; married, May 17, 1883, Ella A. Merrifield, of Sanford, Me.

1547. II. SUSAN L.,[7] born May 8, 1867; married, May 17, 1885, Elmer W. Rogers, of Rochester, N. H.

1548. III. MINNIE A.,[7] born December 17, 1870.

1549. IV. ELECTRA G.,[7] born May 21, 1873.

1550. V. FRANCIS H.,[7] born December 18, 1875.

1551. VI. JENNIE R.,[7] born June 18, 1878.

1552. VII. MABEL E.,[7] born December 6, 1882.

1553. VI. WILLIS H.,[6] born in Sanford, November

3, 1840; married, January 20, 1866, first, Jennie Roberts, of Lyman, died August 16, 1866; second, Lucinda (Heard) Butler, died November 19, 1873.

1554. IV. MARY,[5] born in Sanford, February 4, 1803; married John F. Stone, of Michigan. Lives in Wayland, Allegan County, Mich.

1555. V. EUNICE,[5] born in Sanford, August 2, 1804; married Rev. Joseph (Thomas?) Greenhalgh, and lives in Auburn, Me.; had:

1556. I. MOSES B.[6] GREENHALGH, married, first, Dorcas Boston. Second, Elizabeth Welland, both of Sanford, Me.; had:

1557. I. CORA A.[7] GREENHALGH.

1558. II. SARAH M.[6] GREENHALGH, married B. A. Adams, of Hampden; had:

a. I. B. G.[7] ADAMS.

1559. III. TIMOTHY[6] GREENHALGH, married twice; had one child.

1560. IV. JAMES[6] GREENHALGH, married Margaret Sawyer, of Portland, Me.; had:

1561. I. WOODBURY H.[7] GREENHALGH.

1562. II. FLORENCE B.[7] GREENHALGH.

1563. III. EDITH H.[7] GREENHALGH.

1564. V. JOSEPH[6] GREENHALGH, married Margaret Miller.

1565. VI. CHARLES B.[6] GREENHALGH, married Mehitable McKenzie; they had one child.

1566. VII. MARY F.[6] GREENHALGH, married C. W Hill; had:

1567. I. S.[7] HILL.

1568. VIII. SUSAN G.[6] GREENHALGH, married Charles Palmer, of Bangor; had:

1569. I. FRED. S.[7] PALMER.

1570. II. CHARLES[7] PALMER.

1571. III. C. R.[7] PALMER.

1572. IV. RANDOLPH B.[7] PALMER.

1573. V. STANLEY[7] PALMER.

1574. IX. JOHN F.[6] GREENHALGH, died in Colorado.

1575. X. ABBIE F.[6] GREENHALGH, married T. W. Holden.

1576. VI. JOSEPH,[5] born April 19 (9?), 1806; married Lydia Shakley; lives in Shapleigh, Me.

1577. VII. LOVE,[5] born January 15, 1808; married, August 26, 1827, John P. Hubbard, of South Berwick; had:

1578. I. MARY E.[6] HUBBARD, born in South Berwick, October 4, 1828; married, April 10, 1850, John Simpson; had:

1579. I. OLIVE E.[7] SIMPSON, born September 3, 1851; married, August 22, 1883, Henry E. Noyes; had:

1580. I. EDITH GERTRUDE[8] NOYES, born January 9, 1885.

1581. II. NANCY ISABELLE[7] SIMPSON, born May 18, 1853; married, May 17, 1877, George B. Cook; had:

1582. I. JOHN[8] COOK, born January 19, 1879.

1583. II. ROGER[8] COOK, born May 15, 1882; died April 22, 1883.

1584. III. CARRIE MAY[8] COOK, born August 23, 1884.

1585. III. CARRIE EMMA[7] SIMPSON, born May 28, 1855; married William E. Rowe. She died August 2, 1884; had:

1586. I. FANNIE[8] ROWE, born November 18, 1874; died April, 1875.

1587. II. WILLIAM B.[8] ROWE, born September 1, 1878.

1588. IV. CHARLES SUMNER[7] SIMPSON, born April 23, 1857.

1589. V. JOHN FRANK[7] SIMPSON, born July 17, 1859.

1590. VI. MARY ELLA[7] SIMPSON, born May 30, 1861.

1591. VII. GEORGE ALBERT[7] SIMPSON, born May 6, 1863.

1592. VIII. HENRIETTA[7] SIMPSON, born September 27, 1865; died November 5, 1865.

1593. IX. ANN GERTRUDE[7] SIMPSON, born July 9, 1867; died April 8, 1883.

1594. II. PAUL R.[6] HUBBARD, born February 25, 1830.

1595. III. ABIGAIL E.[6] HUBBARD, born April 28, 1832.

1596. IV. MOSES[6] HUBBARD, born April 17, 1834.

1597. V. ALBERT H.[6] HUBBARD, born January 25, 1836; was killed in battle of Coffeeville, Miss., December 1, 1862.

1598. VI. SARAH ANN[6] HUBBARD, born February 18, 1840; died August 23, 1866.

1599. VII. George H.[6] Hubbard, born February 20, 1845; died at Port Royal, S. C., November 17, 1861.

1600. VIII. Moses,[5] born in Sanford, January 21, 1810; married, February 16, 1834, Joanna Ricker. He was appointed deputy sheriff for York County, Me., in 1832, and subsequently served as justice for five years. Lives in South Acton, Me. ; had :

1601. I. Ann Elizabeth,[6] born August 7, 1835; married, October 2, 1853, Samuel W. Foss; had :

1602. I. Charles W.[7] Foss, born July 25, 1857.

1603. II. William H.[7] Foss, born April 12, 1860.

1604. II. Abbie P.,[6] born September 2, 1836 ; married, October 2, 1859, John Hatch ; had :

1605. I. Grace M.[7] Hatch, born November 4, 1861.

1606. II. Mary A.[7] Hatch, born February 22, 1863.

1607. III. Lucius M.[7] Hatch, born August 5, 1865.

1608. IV. Albert E.[7] Hatch, born November 16, 1867.

1609. V. Gertrude F.[7] Hatch, born March 30, 1870.

1610. VI. Alida E.[7] Hatch, born March 31, 1873.

1611. III. Hannah M.,[6] born December 26, 1838; married, June 17, 1855, Charles H. Fernald ; had :

1612. I. Charles N.[7] Fernald, born August 23, 1856 ; died young.

1613. II. Amos[7] Fernald, born October 5, 1857; died January 20, 1869.

1614. III. Carrie A.[7] Fernald, born November 15, 1863.

1615. IV. Gertrude L.[7] Fernald, born December 26, 1867 ; died young.

1616. V. Herbert B.[7] Fernald, born March 27, 1872.

1617. VI. Charles E.[7] Fernald, born January 18, 1874.

1618. IV. Mary R.,[6] born January 9, 1841; died young.

1619. V. Moses Jordan,[6] born May 5, 1843; died May 29, 1876; married June 6, 1869, Alice R. Doane.

1620. VI. Nathaniel L.,[6] born June 29, 1845; married, September 5, 1877, Mary E. Bodsell.

1621. VII. Joanna S.,[6] born August 6, 1847; died May 9, 1859.

a. VIII. John R.,[6] born August 30, 1849; married September 22, 1870, Etta M. Hilton.

1622. IX. Charles E.,[6] born March 4, 1852; died February 9, 1853.

1623. X. Henry E.,[6] born May 13, 1855; died February 6, 1859.

1624. XI. Clarence A.,[6] born February 2, 1858; is a teacher in Dakota.

Moses [4] (71) had by his second wife, Mary Pray, whom he married in 1811:

1625. IX. Abigail,[5] born July 10, 1812; married William Morseman, and lives in Wakefield, Mass.

1626. X. CHARLES,[5] born October 31, 1813; married, first, January 9, 1840, Dorcas Carroll. Again, June 16, 1860, Ann Lord, and lives in Sanford, Me.; had, by first wife, Dorcas:

1627. I. LUTHER H.,[6] born December 13, 1840; married, November 24, 1867, Lelia G. Ross; had:

1628. I. CLARENCE E.,[7] born April 1, 1869.

1629. II. GEORGE W.,[6] born December 13, 1845; married, June 9, 1870, Mary A. Libby; had:

1630. I. EDITH M.,[7] born October 30, 1871.

1631. II. HAVEN S.,[7] born November 27, 1873.

1632. III. MARTHA E.,[7] born October 15, 1877.

1633. III. FRANK N.,[6] born September 15, 1851.

1634. IV. CHARLES W.,[6] born August 2, 1854; died May 9, 1877.

1635. XI. DORCAS,[5] born December 17, 1814; married, September 29, 1836, Harrison Beal, and lives in Avon, Me.; had:

1636. I. ADELINE[6] BEAL, born March 22, 1838; married, August 27, 1868, Russell N. Thomas; had:

1637. I. IDA B.[7] THOMAS, born April 14, 1869.

1638. II. LEON[7] THOMAS, born February 1, 1877.

1639. II. LUTHER[6] BEAL, born September 2, 1840; married, August 14, 1872, Abbie Pease; had:

1640. I. FLORA E.[7] BEAL, born June 10, 1873.

1641. II. HERMAN J.[7] BEAL, born July 17, 1876.

1642. III. GEORGE F.[6] BEAL, born January 28, 1845, married, July 4, 1870, Alma M. Brown.

11

1643. IV. Oliver J.[6] Beal, born July 27, 1848;
married, May 10, 1868, Daniel H. Crosley;
had :

1644. I. Clara E.[7] Crosley, born May 26, 1871.

1645. V. Laura E.[6] Beal, born January 20, 1851;
married, June 28, 1874, Frederick A. Bright;
had :

1646. I. Bertie N.[7] Bright, born April 28, 1875.

1647. VI. Clara E.[6] Beal, born October 10, 1855.

1648. XII. Olive,[5] born February 29, 1816; married, August 2, 1834, Alden Quint, born
January 30, 1810. He was son of Joseph
and Hannah (Roberts) Quint. They lived
in Sanford, Me.; had :

1649. I. Charles M.[6] Quint, born May 7, 1835;
married, September 8, 1866, Maria Burroughs,
born in Stafford, Vt., December 23, 1847;
had :

1650. I. Angie Belle[7] Quint, born March 24,
1868.

1651. II. Charles Alden[7] Quint, born January
12, 1870.

1652. III. Joseph Sumner[7] Quint, born April 28,
1872.

1653. IV. Olive Rebecca[7] Quint, born September
25, 1873.

1654. V. Annie Maria[7] Quint, born June 29,
1875.

1655. II. Hannah Rebecca[6] Quint, born October
17, 1842; married, January 16, 1868, Samuel

Ham Garvin, of Acton, Me.; born May 10, 1842. He was one of the Selectmen for Acton in 1877.

1656. XIII. LYMAN,[5] born September 19, 1817. He has served as a Representative in the State Legislature. Married, October 19, 1841, Cynthia Webber, and lives in Sanford, Me.; had :

1657. I. ELLEN L.,[6] born April 4, 1843 ; married —— Giles, of Great Falls, N. H.; had :

1658. I. ELMER E.[7] GILES, born in Great Falls, N. H., 1862.

1659. II. NELLIE B.[7] GILES, born in 1863 ; died, 1867.

1660. III. WILLIAM C.[7] GILES, born in Great Falls, 1865.

1661. II. CHARLES F.,[6] born March 25, 1845 ; died December 25, 1863.

1662. III. MARIETTA,[6] born April 23, 1847 ; married —— Porter ; had :

1663. I. ERNEST B.[7] PORTER, born 1872 ; died young.

1664. II. JOSIE B.[7] PORTER, born 1873.

1665. III. DANA W.[7] PORTER, born 1875.

1666. IV. MARIETTA[7] PORTER, born 1877.

1667. IV. ABBIE A.,[6] born July 23, 1849.

1668. V. LYMAN,[6] born August 20, 1851 ; died young.

1669. VI. ADELINE F.,[6] born January 21, 1854 ; married —— Metzger, of Lynn, Mass.; had :

1670. I. BUTLER [7] METZGER, born 1874.

1671. II. JAY [7] METZGER, born 1876.

1672. VII. ANSON M.,[6] born May 3, 1856.

1673. VIII. LYMAN A.,[6] born July 6, 1860.

1674. IX. ADDIE M.,[6] born November 8, 1862.

1675. X. HIRAM A.,[6] born July 11, 1865.

1676. XIV. LUCRETIA,[5] born February 14, 1819; married, November 23, 1837, Albra Morrison, and lived in Sanford, Me.; had:

1677. I. GEORGE H.[6] MORRISON, born October 21, 1839; died July 9, 1840.

1678. II. SUSAN A.[6] MORRISON, born August 11, 1841.

1679. III. HEBRON L.[6] MORRISON, born August 16, 1843.

1680. IV. CHARLES W.[6] MORRISON, born June 4, 1845; married, first, May 6, 1863, Mary McCann; had:

1681. I. FLORA E.[7] MORRISON, born July 21, 1864.

1682. II. LEONARD F.[7] MORRISON, born March 10, 1868.

1683. III. MABEL E.[7] MORRISON, born March 16, 1872.

Married again Emma McCann.

1684. V. GEORGE M.[6] MORRISON, born January 12, 1847; married, January 1, 1870, ——— Roberts; had:

1685. I. LULU A.[7] MORRISON, born September 28, 1876.

1686. VI. MARY A.[6] MORRISON, born October 19

1848 ; married Daniel S. Cheney, of Danvers, Mass.

1687. VII. MARTHA A.[6] MORRISON, born July 16, 1850 ; married, May 22, 1870, Charles Roberts, of Danvers ; had :

1688. I. ELLA[7] ROBERTS, born February 1, 1873.

1689. VIII. EMMA P.[6] MORRISON, born May 15, 1852 ; married, November 25, 1872, Charles Cavano, of Dover, N. H.

1690. IX. ELVA A.[6] MORRISON, born March 9, 1854 ; married, September 25, 1873, Wesley Ross, of Springvale, Me.

1691. X. ALMA B.[6] MORRISON, born March 25 1856; married, February 7, 1874, Richard Bradbury ; died July 5, 1877.

1692. XI. ANSEL H.[6] MORRISON, born March 9, 1858.

1693. XV. WENTWORTH,[5] born July 16, 1820 ; died September 18, 1820.

1694. XVI. WENTWORTH[5] again, born May 16, 1822. Went from home and has never been heard from.

1695. XVII. HIRAM P.,[5] born in Sanford, January 10, 1825 ; married, first, March 17, 1851, Adeline McClellan ; married again, March 15, 1864, Lizzie Hodsdon. He had by first wife :

1696. I. IDA,[6] born in Mendon, Mass., April 6, 1852.

1697. II. JAMES M.,[6] born in Mendon, July 8, 1854.

1698. III. ALBERT E.,[6] born in Mendon, October 5, 1865.

1699. IV. LENA E.,[6] born in Mendon, October 8, 1871.

1700. V. SUMNER,[6] born in Mendon, September 20, 1875.

72.

JAMES[4] BUTLER, fifth child of Charles[3] and Sarah (Cross) Butler; married, April 25, 1802, Olive Earl. They lived at first in Sanford and afterward in South Berwick, Me.; had:

1701. I. ABIGAIL,[5] born December 15, 1802.

1702. II. GILBERT,[5] born June 23, 1805; died young.

1703. III. GILBERT,[5] born July 22, 1808; died June 12, 1866; married, first, about 1838, Sarah Jellison, born August 11, 1819, died September 11, 1858; had:

1704. I. ABBY J.,[6] born January 2, 1840; died February 25, 1857.

1705. II. CHARLES,[6] born April 6, 1842; died February 1, 1868.

He married again, August 15, 1860, Sarah Walker, born December 19, 1825, died January 6, 1883; had:

1706. III. ALTON G.,[6] born July 29, 1861.

1707. IV. CHARLES,[5] born with Gilbert, July 22, 1808.

1708. V. FREDERICK,[5] born February 23, 1811.

1709. VI. SARAH,[5] born December 6, 1814; married Cyrus Elwell; had:

1710. I. WASHINGTON.[6]
1711. II. WATSON [6] ELWELL, twins.
1712. III. OLIVE [6] ELWELL.
1713. IV. SOPHIA [6] ELWELL.
1714. V. CHARLES [6] ELWELL.
1715. VI. FRANK [6] ELWELL.
1716. VII. ELIZABETH,[5] born February 22, 1818; died single.
1717. VIII. JAMES,[5] born January 6, 1821.
1718. IX. OLIVE,[5] born 1823; married Daniel Stone, and died without issue, September 8, 1860.

73.

LOVE [4] BUTLER, sixth child of Charles [3] and Sarah (Cross) Butler, born in South Berwick; married, June 18, 1795, Jedediah Jenkins; had:

1719. I. SARAH [5] JENKINS.
1720. II. MARY [5] JENKINS.
　　　 III. LYDIA [5] JENKINS.
　　　 IV. HANNAH [5] JENKINS.

74.

SARAH [4] BUTLER, seventh child of Charles [3] and Sarah (Cross) Butler, born in South Berwick, February 12, 1775; married, November 5, 1800, Wentworth Chadbourne, son of Scammon and Hannah (Guptill) Chadbourne; had:

1721. I. HANNAH [5] CHADBOURNE, born December 17, 1801.
1722. II. EBENEZER [5] CHADBOURNE (Col.), born

July 27, 1806; lived in Berwick, and died
without issue.
1723. III. MARY[5] CHADBOURNE, born September 9,
1801; died April, 1834.

75.

NANCY[4] BUTLER, eighth child of Charles[3] and
Sarah (Cross) Butler, born in Berwick, Me.; married Moses Roberts (certificate given October 25,
1800); had:
1724. I. SOPHIA[5] ROBERTS, born in South Berwick.
1725. II. CHARLES[5] ROBERTS.
1726. III. SABINA[5] ROBERTS.
1727. IV. ABIGAIL[5] ROBERTS.
1728. V. SALLY[5] ROBERTS.
1729. VI. NANCY[5] ROBERTS.

76.

ABIGAIL[4] BUTLER, ninth child of Charles[3] and
Sarah (Cross) Butler, born in South Berwick,
October 2, 1791; married, first, James Murray,
and second, Joseph Littlefield; had:
1730. I. RHODA[5] MURRAY.
1731. II. SALLY[5] MURRAY.
1732. III. NANCY[5] MURRAY.
1733. IV. HANNAH[5] MURRAY.
1734. V. CHARLES[5] MURRAY.
1735. VI. SOPHIA[5] MURRAY.
1736. VII. THEDOSIA[5] MURRAY.
1737. VIII. GEORGE[5] MURRAY.

INDEX.

SURNAMES OF BUTLER.

INDEX.

OTHER SURNAMES THAN BUTLER.

```
```

```
```

PAGE

Freeland, Ida Augusta 35
 James M.............. 36
 J. M. C.............. 35
 James Pleasant........ 36
 Joseph F............. 35
 Julia Clayton 36
 Julia C............. 36
 Leroy M............. 37
 Mamie Lee 36
 Mary Frances 36
 Nehemiah K.......... 37
 Robert F 35
 Sarah Augusta 36
 Sanford Eugene....... 35
 Walter Butler........ 37
 Walter Randolph..... 36
 Willis Eugene........ 36
 William 37
 William E 35
Freeman, Elizabeth W 34
 Henrietta............ 39
 Henry F............. 39
 Sarah M 81
Frisbee, Almira F 100
Frost, Betsey 108
 James................ 141
 Nancy (Davis)......... 141
Fuller, Carrie May........ 95
 Charles F............ 95
 Grace L 95
 John F.............. 95
Furbush, Rachel 98
Furber, Elizabeth 148
 Jethro............... 112
 Rose 112

Garvin, Samuel Ham....... 163
Gayman, George 144
Gerrish, Bridget 21
 Frank H............. 132
 Isaac, Jr............. 138
Giles, Elmer E 163
 Jennie M............. 152
 Nellie B............. 163
 William C........... 163
Gilman, William Edward.. 86
Greenhalgh, Abbie F...... 157
 Charles B........... 156

PAGE

Greenhalgh, Cora A....... 156
 Edith H............. 156
 Florence 156
 James 156
 John F.............. 157
 Joseph 156
 Rev. Joseph.......... 156
 Mary F............. 156
 Moses B 156
 Sarah M............ 156
 Susan G............ 157
 (Thomas ?).......... 156
 Timothy............ 156
 Woodbury 156
Gilpatrick, Benjamin 52
 John H............. 52
 Rev. Joseph 155
 Luella 52
 Sarah 52
Gibson, Vinnie, m. Edmund
 Andrews 47
Goodwin, Abigail.......... 153
 Albert H............ 50
 Albert T............ 49
 Alice 50
 Almeda............. 77
 Alvin J............. 137
 Ann................ 153
 Betsy 49
 Charles R........... 50
 Christiana B......... 77
 Clara E............ 72
 Cora B............. 50
 Daniel............10, 115
 Eliza.............45, 115
 Fanny 77, 97
 Gideon 11
 Harry Horner 137
 Hiram 72
 Henry 10
 Harriet 71
 Harriet S........... 72
 Joseph 71
 Lizzie 73
 Lorenzo D.......... 77
 Loring 77
 Lydia 48
 Mahala 153

www.ingramcontent.com/pod-product-compliance
Lightning Source LLC
Chambersburg PA
CBHW072227270326
41930CB00010B/2022

* 9 7 8 1 5 5 6 1 3 2 4 1 4 *